Nifty Knits for Kids

Fun Wearables for Kids on the Go

Nifty Knits for Kids

Fun Wearables for Kids on the Go

By Catherine Ham

LARK BOOKS
A Division of Sterling Publishing Co., Inc.
New York

EDITOR
Joanne O'Sullivan

ART DIRECTOR
Stacey Budge

COVER DESIGNER
Cindy LaBreacht

ASSOCIATE EDITOR
Susan Kieffer

ASSOCIATE ART DIRECTOR
Lance Wille

ART PRODUCTION ASSISTANT
Jeff Hamilton

EDITORIAL ASSISTANCE
Delores Gosnell

EDITORIAL INTERN
Katrina Usher

ART INTERN
Marshall Hudson

ILLUSTRATOR
Orrin Lundgren

PHOTOGRAPHER
www.wrightcreativeinc.com

Dedication

FOR JULIA AND LUCIA

Library of Congress Cataloging-in-Publication Data

Ham, Catherine.
 Nifty knits for kids : fun wearables for kids on the go /
by Catherine Ham. -- 1st ed.
    p. cm.
 Includes index.
 ISBN 1-57990-851-9 (hardcover)
 1. Knitting--Patterns. 2. Children's clothing. I. Title.
 TT825.H356 2007
 746.43'20432--dc22

                        2006029697

10 9 8 7 6 5 4 3 2 1

First Edition

Published by Lark Books, A Division of
Sterling Publishing Co., Inc.
387 Park Avenue South, New York, N.Y. 10016

Text © 2007, Catherine Ham
Photography © 2007, Lark Books
Illustrations © 2007, Lark Books

Distributed in Canada by Sterling Publishing,
c/o Canadian Manda Group, 165 Dufferin Street
Toronto, Ontario, Canada M6K 3H6

Distributed in the United Kingdom by GMC Distribution Services,
Castle Place, 166 High Street, Lewes, East Sussex, England BN7 1XU

Distributed in Australia by Capricorn Link (Australia) Pty Ltd.,
P.O. Box 704, Windsor, NSW 2756 Australia

If you have questions or comments about this book, please contact:
Lark Books
67 Broadway
Asheville, NC 28801
(828) 253-0467

Manufactured in China

ISBN 13: 978-1-57990-851-5
ISBN 10: 1-57990-851-9

For information about custom editions, special sales, premium and corporate purchases, please contact Sterling Special Sales Department at 800-805-5489 or specialsales@sterlingpub.com.

CONTENTS

INTRODUCTION

Knitting for kids is very rewarding. Choosing the design, the yarns, and the embellishments is great fun in itself, but greater still is the satisfaction of creating an item that a child will love and a parent will appreciate.

The 30-plus projects in this book were developed with four basic principles in mind: practicality, comfort, versatility, and fun. Knitwear is very practical for youngsters because it stretches with them as they move and play. But it's not just for winter warmth. Yarns of varying weights and types were used to create season-spanning pieces that a child can wear most of the year. Many of the patterns use details such as ribbon ties that can be adjusted to fit an ever-growing child. (I well remember how frustrating it was to have a child's favorite garment outgrown in a flash.) Comfort is very important in kids' clothes, so shapes were kept simple, allowing garments to be pulled on and off in a snap.

I've also made versatility an essential element of this book. Many of the pieces can be layered over shirts and tees or under jackets and are suitable for both boys and girls. You'll find items that are casual as well as dressy, with lots of options to express individuality to suit the occasion. Cheerful colors and lively use of buttons, beads, ribbons, and pockets make the clothes fun to look at as well as wear, ensuring kids will pick them from the closet every time. As a bonus, several of the projects make good use of yarn oddments, giving you an opportunity to exercise your creativity and produce something unique

It's my hope that the projects in this book will appeal to knitters of many levels, from the newbie with a basic knowledge of knitting, to the more experienced lover of the craft. Knitting for children gives you a great opportunity to try something new, such as stranded colorwork on a little Fair Isle vest (page 46). Don't be afraid to mix and match details from some designs with others. The pockets on the Bugsy Scarf (page 53) can easily be applied to a sweater or jacket, or you could try the exposed seams of the Top of the Class Sweater (page 30) on other knitted garments. Ask yourself: "What if?" There are endless possibilities to do your own thing, and that's one of the great delights of knitting.

I very much enjoyed knitting for my daughters when they were little. Children love getting new clothes and are thrilled if something has been made especially for them. Whoever the lucky child is that you're knitting for, I hope you'll enjoy trying out some of these designs.

Happy knitting!

Getting Started

ONE OF THE THINGS I love about knitting is that there's always something new to learn—some little way to improve your technique, and by so doing, make your work neater or easier. It's amazing how a knitter can be quite skilled in one technique, but perhaps only just beginning to learn another. In this section of the book, I hope to provide information that will help you advance as a knitter, whatever your current level. Complete beginners will need to refer to an introduction to knitting. Each pattern indicates the skill level required to knit it, but this is only a guide—don't be afraid to tackle a particular project just because the word experienced appears on the page. Read through the pattern first (something you should always do), and you may find that you can handle it very well indeed. The patterns are not complex; none of them is written for advanced knitters.

Designing for Kids

Clothing for kids should be loose and comfortable, easy to take on and off. The designs presented in this book have simple shapes and comfy necklines. Cuffs and hems are somewhat loose and unrestricted. Sleeves aren't baggy—those can make movement awkward and possibly even dangerous if they should catch on something. Yarns have been chosen for reasonably quick knitting, but they aren't excessively heavy or bulky for the active child.

Clothing that can be worn in layers is ideal for kids, because it gives more options for mix 'n' match outfits. The three-piece set on page 90 can be worn in a variety of ways, and it will be a useful part of a little girl's wardrobe through at least three seasons. The vest will fit from jacket length to just on the waist as the child grows, giving you good value for your time and money. Several of the sweater projects are suitable for both girls and boys, and others offer a sweater or vest option, such as the Busy Bee set on page 103.

I love bright colors for kids—the brighter the colors, the more options for pairing a piece with shirts, tees, and pants. Let the child who will be wearing the item choose the colors if you can, and respect his or her choices.

Kids' Sizing

Children of the same age vary so much in shape and size that it's not always possible to choose a size based on age. Measure the child's chest, if the child is available, or ask the parent/caregiver to do so. Allow at least 4 inches (10 cm) of wearing ease for freedom of movement, and use the finished chest measurements of the pattern to select which size to knit. You can then adjust the finished sleeve and body length if necessary. Knitting the sleeves longer allows the sleeve to be cuffed, which will also provide extra warmth until the child grows. At the same time, bear in mind that if you knit an excessively large size, it may not be appropriate for the season by the time the child fits into it.

Some of the designs in the book have ribbon ties, which allow you to adjust the length to the growing child. Kids tend to grow taller more quickly than they grow wider. Where possible, the garments have been designed so that the sleeves are worked down from the shoulder, such as the sweaters on pages 38, 42, and 50. Several of the tops (pages 22, 75, and 96) can be worn alone in warmer weather, or layered on cooler days, while the sweater dress on page 69 will become a sweater as the young lady grows.

Yarns

The world of knitting yarns is a wondrously exciting one, full of the most fabulous delights and temptations, and oh-so-hard to resist. We knitters can get quite carried away discussing yarn, but to stay focused, I'll just discuss yarns suitable for children's garments.

If you frequently knit for children, you probably have some favorite yarns that you're comfortable with. Many knitters will use only cotton or acrylics to make kids' clothes; others swear by wool or wool blends. Each of these yarn types has its advantages. Yarn choices for kids are usually made with cost and laundry issues in mind, as most people don't want to drop a bundle of money to knit something that will be outgrown very quickly or that might require special laundering. If the garment is going to be passed along to family and friends, though, consider a yarn of reasonably good quality to ensure that it wears well. Yarn manufacturers are sensitive to these issues, and produce many excellent and inexpensive yarns that are ideal for kids' knitwear, so it shouldn't be a problem to find something to suit your needs. Check your local yarn store or the Internet for advice and opinions about specific yarns.

Cheap yarn and yarn bought inexpensively are not necessarily the same thing. It's amazing what you can find in the sale bins of yarn stores, especially as these tend to contain just a few balls of a particular yarn (kiddie knits don't usually require large amounts). The discount coupons from craft and hobby stores can also offer incredible deals on yarn.

The patterns in the book indicate the approximate yardage needed to knit the item, but bear in mind that you may need more if you decide to lengthen the garment or the sleeves, and that yardage requirements will probably be affected if you use a different yarn.

YARN SUBSTITUTIONS

Most knitters could write a book, or at least a chapter or two, on this subject! The reasons for needing to use a different yarn are many. Knitters may wish to use a substitute yarn because they prefer its particular qualities, the cost of the suggested yarn is too expensive, or the specified yarn is not available. Yarn manufacturers are constantly offering new and ever more fabulous yarns. Just as frequently, they withdraw certain yarns. Canny knitters know from experience that "yarn today, but not tomorrow" is a reality, and they make a point of stocking up on their favorite yarns. This is known in the knitterhood as "building up a stash" and is the mark of a prudent knitter.

Substituting one yarn for another is fairly easy to do, but you'll still need to take a few issues into consideration before proceeding. The pattern itself will offer several clues. What, in particular, has caught your eye? The shape? The style? The texture of the yarn? Is it smooth, or does it have surface interest? Are there design details, such as cables or lace sections that might well lose their impact if the substitute yarn has a different

hand and texture from the original choice? Cables knit in very soft yarns or fluffy mohairs will look quite different from cables knit in tweed yarns, which have much more body and will define the cable stitches clearly. Not only that, but the finished garment, which may be very beautiful in the substitute yarn, will not look the same as the one knitted in the rugged tweed. The drape, or way the knitted fabric falls on the body, may well be different from what the designer intended. At best, this might change the way you decide to wear it; at worst, you could well be disappointed if, after all your work and high expectations, the item doesn't look as you'd hoped. But then again, you might be able to carry it all off with great style!

The way the yarn is spun must also be considered. A smooth mercerized cotton will knit up differently than a cotton bouclé, while a tightly plied wool will result in a fabric very different from one knitted in a loosely spun, more lofty yarn. Color, too, plays a role that might not seem obvious at first. The Fair Isle Vest on page 46 illustrates this point. Only two colors are used in the body of the vest, but note that one of these is a variegated yarn, which makes the design look more colorful, and therefore more intricate, than it really is. There's no reason why this vest may not be knitted in two solid colors, and if they work well together the result will surely be pleasing, but the variegated yarn certainly adds that little something extra.

Once you've noted the pattern details, it's time to read the ball band or wrapper—it has a great deal to tell you. Here you'll discover whether the yarn you're considering is pure wool or a blend; perhaps it's acrylic; maybe it's cotton. This can matter a great deal. Cotton, although it has many excellent properties, behaves differently from wool. It does not "remember" well (like some children!), and this makes it very inclined to create holes when working color patterns such as Fair Isle or intarsia. The result is that your knitting, no matter how well done, is likely to look rather untidy. Cotton is heavier than wool and tends to stretch, sometimes very badly, whereas wool and wool blends keep their shape much better.

The ball band will list the manufacturer's suggested gauge, and this information is very important. It's possible that your substitute yarn specifies a stitch and row gauge which precisely corresponds to that of the original yarn. But before you start clapping, consider what we've already discussed in terms of suitability of the yarn for the project. If all continues to sound great, then it's time to knit a gauge swatch (see page 12).

The ball band should list the number of yards in the ball. If you have this information, it's a simple matter to calculate how many balls or skeins you'll need to knit the item. The pattern will specify the amount of yarn used in each color and type; divide the number of yards in a ball of the yarn you're considering into the total yardage requirements given for the pattern, and you'll know roughly how many balls are required. Bear in mind that specified yarn amounts will vary slightly because knitters differ in the way they knit. That's about all there is to it—it's really no biggie if you remember the basic pointers. What's more, you'll have fun while you learn a great deal about yarns and their characteristics as you test new ones and ask yourself, "What if ... ?"

GAUGE

The importance of checking your gauge cannot be overstated. It's like test-driving a car to see what you can expect from it. In the same way, you need to see how the yarn behaves, how it feels in your hands, and what results you'll get from it. The gauge swatch is your seatbelt—it can keep you out of a lot of trouble. Once you've selected the yarn and needles, cast on a minimum of 20 stitches—preferably more—and knit a swatch of at least 4 inches(10cm). Before you measure it, handle the piece to decide whether it feels good enough against the skin to wear comfortably. Does it have the right "hand" (texture and drape) for the item you're making?

If you'll be washing the finished garment, wash and dry the gauge swatch first. Lay the swatch on a flat surface, place pins to indicate where you'll start measuring, and measure it (I use a clear plastic ruler), carefully counting the number of stitches in exactly 4 inches (10 cm).

Measure without stretching the knitting, and don't include the edge stitches, which easily distort. If your gauge differs from that given in your pattern by even a fraction of an inch, your finished piece may be significantly larger or smaller than it should be, which could be quite devastating. If your gauge swatch is too big, try again on smaller needles. Use bigger needles if your swatch is smaller than it should be. Keep testing until you are satisfied with the results. Don't overlook row gauge. While it's not always crucial to the fit in a style with little shaping (such as a tank top or a drop shoulder style) it can't just be ignored. If your row gauge differs considerably from that specified in the pattern, you may find that your sleeves reach the desired length before the increases are complete or before you have worked all the decreases needed to narrow the sleeve. The height of a sleeve cap is dependent on row gauge, and if your substitute yarn doesn't match fairly closely, it could well be that the sleeve cap does not fit the armhole.

It's tempting to skip making a gauge swatch, but you won't regret it. Gauge swatches are not a waste of your time or yarn. Some knitters keep them for future reference; others unravel them and use the yarn again. If you want yours to refer to later, keep a few hangtags (from office supply stores) handy and record the needle size and any other useful information on them. I find swatches helpful when I'm in a hurry to try out a stitch pattern. Instead of binding off when I'm done with a swatch, I leave the stitches on a length of yarn. When I begin experimenting with a pattern stitch, I slip these stitches onto a needle and get a feel for the new stitch first. If it seems promising, I then make a new gauge swatch with the needle size that works best.

Using Patterns and Schematics

Before you begin a project, read through the pattern carefully to familiarize yourself with what you'll be doing. Pattern instructions are usually given in a range of sizes. Determine which size you want to use and mark it in some way to highlight your requirements. If you'd rather not mark the pattern itself, photocopy it, then mark it up. Photocopies are also useful so you don't have to carry a whole book around with you. To determine the size you're going to knit, check the measurements given for the garment in the pattern or on the schematic (which in this book, is provided for you). The schematic, a diagram of the finished piece with all the measurements indicated, is not something to ignore or panic about. It's very helpful in showing you at a glance how the knitted pieces will look. It also gives the finished lengths, so you can decide in advance whether you want to adjust the body or sleeve lengths. Keep a record of any changes you make should you want to knit the item again later. Also, for future reference, make a note of what gauge you achieved with a particular yarn and what size needles you used.

USING MARKERS AND STITCH HOLDERS

If you're a fairly new knitter, you may not have needed to use markers before. These handy little devices are placed to mark a particular point in the knitting, such as the beginning of a round, the position of the sleeves, places to pick up stitches, or places to add buttons. Knitting supply stores sell all kinds of markers, and knitters have their favorite types. Safety pins work well for this purpose; even bent paper clips or small loops of a different colored yarn will do.

Stitch holders are used to hold groups of stitches that are not being worked but will be needed later. As with markers, various types are available. Spare knitting needles are suitable for this, and it's a good idea to use some kind of end stop to ensure that the stitches don't slip off the needle. A rubber band can be wrapped around the needle for this. Lengths of smooth yarn work well to hold stitches. Thread a tapestry needle with the holding yarn, take the stitches off the knitting needle onto the yarn, and then tie a knot to secure the stitches.

Techniques

As mentioned previously, we won't delve into the basic how-to of knitting here—you'll need an introduction to knitting for that. Instead, we'll cover some of the techniques you'll need to know to work the projects in this book.

CIRCULAR KNITTING (KNITTING IN-THE-ROUND)

Knitting on a circular needle of the appropriate length, or on a set of double-pointed needles, produces a seamless tube of knitted fabric. (You may see instructions telling you to change from a circular needle to a set of double points when the stitches are decreased to the stage where they can no longer fit around the circular needle.) Circular knitting has a great many advantages, not the least of which is that it eliminates the need for seams. You cast the stitches onto the circular needle in the usual way and then join them into a round. You must take care here to ensure that the stitches aren't twisted on the needle; then use the right-hand needle to knit the first stitch off the left-hand needle, pulling the stitches tightly together at the beginning of the round. You place a marker to indicate the beginning of the round—then round and round you go, usually working in the knit stitch only.

There are knitters who will do pretty much anything to avoid knitting flat pieces, that is to say, knitting back and forth in rows. There are knitters who are equally determined to avoid knitting in the round. Both methods have their place. If, however, you haven't yet tried circular knitting, do give it a go. For more information on this wonderful method of knitting, refer to a basic knitting text.

Note: Circular needles are great for knitting flat pieces; they're not only for knitting in the round.

THREE-NEEDLE BIND-OFF

This simple and brilliantly effective technique saves time and results in a less bulky seam with a very neat appearance. It's a particularly useful method of binding off and simultaneously joining shoulder seams. An added advantage is that the seam is very strong, making it ideal for children's knits, which are often subjected to hard wear.

Just as its name suggests, three needles are used. The two sets of stitches to be bound off are held on needles or stitch holders until they are needed. Place the stitches back onto the needles, with the right sides together and the points of the needles facing in the same direction. I prefer to use a needle one size larger to bind off with, thus ensuring that the bind-off is not too tight. The bind-off is worked in the usual manner, except that the third needle is inserted into the first stitch on both the needles holding stitches, and are then knit together (fig 1). Repeat for the second set of stitches on each needle. You'll have two stitches on the right-hand needle (fig. 2). Pass the first stitch over the second (fig. 3), so there's one stitch on the right needle; continue binding off in this way until only one stitch remains, and then fasten off. Ideally, you should have the same number of stitches on each needle when you begin a three-needle bind-off, but if for some reason you don't, you'll need to fudge a little by knitting two stitches together occasionally as needed. It's best to reach the end of the seam with the same number of stitches left on each needle, to avoid an uneven edge on the seam.

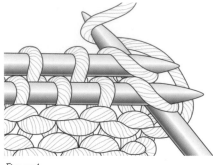
Figure 1

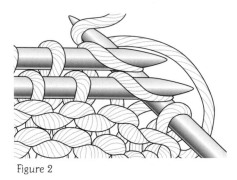
Figure 2

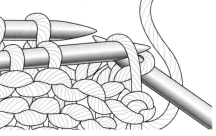
Figure 3

BUTTONS AND BUTTONHOLES

Most knitters love buttons because they can so easily transform a very simple garment or item into something quite special. I just couldn't resist the buttons used in the little two-piece set on page 25 when I saw them in the yarn shop, and the outfit was designed around them. Buttons certainly don't have to be functional, though—there are endless ways to use them for embellishments and decorative effects.

As much as knitters love buttons, though, they are often heard discussing the pros and cons of the buttonhole, which must accompany them. Problems could well arise if a very large button is used in a closure. The beauty of knitted fabric is its elasticity, and an overly large buttonhole may stretch out of shape, unless it's very carefully worked. In such cases, use snaps for the closure and sew the buttons over them.

Abbreviations

If you're unsure about a term or technique check with a knitting friend or turn to one of the many online knitting communities. There's a wealth of resources out there and knitters are always more than willing to share their knowledge.

*	repeat from * as many times as indicated
()	or alternate measurement(s)/stitch counts
alt	alternate
approx	approximately
beg	begin or beginning
BO	bind off
cm	centimeter(s)
CO	cast on
cont	continue or continuing
dec	decrease or decreasing
dpn	double pointed needle(s)
g	gram
g st	garter stitch
inc	increase or increasing
k	knit
k2tog	knit 2 sts together
M1	make 1 st
m	meter(s)
MC	main color
mm	millimeter(s)
oz	ounce(s)
pat	pattern
p	purl
psso	pass the slipped stitch over
rev St st	reverse stockinette stitch
RS	right side(s)
SC	single crochet
ssk	slip 1 stitch as if to knit, slip 1 stitch as if to knit, then knit these 2 sts together
SK2P	slip 1, knit 2 together, pass the slipped stitch over
st(s)	stitch(es)
St st	stockinette stitch
tbl	through back of loops
tog	together
WS	wrong side(s)
yd	yard(s)
yfd	yarn forward
yo	yarn over

WORKING WITH MIRROR IMAGES

There are many instances in knitting where two pieces are worked as mirror images of each other, as in the case of the right and left fronts of a jacket or cardigan. The pattern will generally give the full instructions for the left or right piece, and then tell you to work the second piece to match the first, reversing all shapings. All this means is that you work the second piece in the opposite way, so, where you decreased for the neck or armhole shaping on the right side of the knitting, you will do so on the left side for the second piece, or the mirror image.

Similarly, when you begin shaping the back or front of a pullover style, you'll need to work the sleeve and neck shapings as mirror images of each other, but now you have one piece of knitting on the needles, not two completely separate halves. Pattern writers will instruct you how to do this in one of two commonly used ways. One method is to work both sides of the neck and/or sleeve shaping at the same time, by joining in a second ball of yarn. The advantage here is that you do to one piece as you do to the other (or should!), so your pieces should match perfectly. For the second length of yarn, you can work from the other end of your ball if you like, rather than using another ball of yarn altogether. (This method has come into hand knitting by way of machine knitting, where it's typically used.)

Refer to a basic knitting book for information on various types of buttonholes. It's worth trying some of these out on a gauge swatch to see which methods you prefer. A simple eyelet has worked well for me on items where a small buttonhole will be sufficient. This is very easy to do—bring the yarn forward and knit two stitches together. If you have forgotten to make a buttonhole, or decide later that you'd like one, the forgiving nature of knitted fabric will work in your favor, provided that you can use a small button. Carefully separate the stitches at the point where you'd like to have a buttonhole and see whether you can wiggle the button through it. With a matching sewing thread or embroidery floss, work buttonhole stitch around the hole. Treat this buttonhole carefully and it should work well.

The second method involves leaving one set of stitches on a holder while you complete working on one side of the knitting. Then you return to the held stitches and work the mirror image. There is no law of knitting that states one method must be used instead of the other. You decide which works best for you.

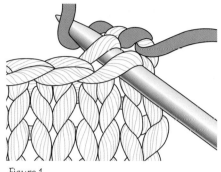
Figure 1

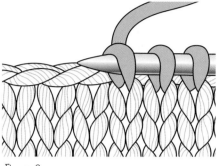
Figure 2

PICKING UP STITCHES

Sweater patterns may call for picking up stitches to place a finished edge on a knitted piece. Sleeve bands on vests, front edge bands on cardigans and jackets, and neckbands are examples. When you're picking up a large number of stitches, circular needles may be necessary, because they come in much longer lengths than straight needles do.

Beautifully finished bands are not difficult to achieve if you follow a few simple steps. First, mark the edges of the knitting where the stitches will be picked up and divide into equal segments. Count the rows between the markers to ensure even spacing. (Safety pins work well as markers, because they won't fall out of the knitting.) With the right side facing you, carefully separate the edge stitches so that you can see the small space, or hole, between each row of knitting. Push the needle through the hole (fig. 1) to the back of the work, place the yarn around the needle as if to knit, and then draw a loop of yarn through with the needle (fig. 2). Continue along the edge in this way, picking up the

stitches at a ratio of three stitches for every four rows. When you've picked up all the stitches, continue knitting the bands in the desired pattern stitch.

Remember that the number of stitches you end up with is dependent on the number of rows in the edge you're picking up from. You may have a different number of rows than the designer did if you've changed the length of the piece or used a different yarn. Knitting styles also affect the gauge. A few stitches more or less doesn't necessarily mean that yours is all wrong. What's important is how the picked-up stitches look and how well they lie against the rest of the knitting. It's difficult to see whether the stitches have been picked up evenly when they're bunched together on the needle.

Unfortunately, some knitters don't check the fit of the garment before completing the finishing. It's very disappointing to find that the neckline fits poorly or that bands don't lie flat, and yet you can easily remedy this problem. Try this method to check the fit: thread a bodkin or a tapestry needle with thread in a contrasting color, and

take the stitches carefully off the knitting needle. Adjust them evenly on this thread so you can see how they will look when bound off. If you have too many stitches, your band will be wavy. If there are too few, it will pull in. Count the stitches and decide how many to add or remove. When you're satisfied, place the stitches back onto the knitting needle and complete the bands.

PUTTING IT ALL TOGETHER

Many of the designs in this book require very little sewing up of seams, and some, such as the Fair Isle Vest on page 46, have no seams at all. Shoulders are joined together in many of the garments with a three-needle bind-off, a technique well worth learning if you don't already know it. Instructions are given in this text for binding off seams together in this way (see page 14), but you'll probably want to refer to your favorite basic knitting text for more detailed information on the subject of seaming knitwear.

Where seams are required in knitting, you usually want them to be as inconspicuous as possible, except where seams are a feature of the design, as in the Top of the Class Sweater on page 30. Here, boldly contrasting exposed seams, worked with a three-needle bind-off at the shoulders and armholes, are used to good effect on an otherwise plain sweater. Turning seams inside out like this is an easy way to add detailing interest to other designs, and you may enjoy experimenting with this technique.

BLOCKING

Considering the time and effort put into your knitting, it's worth taking the time to learn the basic techniques. One of these is the proper preparation of knitted pieces before they're assembled, usually referred to as blocking.

Blocking is the process of smoothing out the knitted pieces to the correct size and shape before you assemble them. I prefer the wet blocking method because it is simple, is safe for all yarns, and always gives me good results. To block a piece of knitting, you'll need to work on a large, flat surface. Blocking boards designed for this purpose are available, or you can work on the floor with a towel under the knitting. Pin the knitted pieces out to the correct shape, using blocking pins. The pins are made of stainless steel so that they won't rust and are available at any good yarn shop. Position the pins at regular intervals all around the edges of the knitting, then check that the pieces are the correct size by

comparing them to the measurements given on the schematic. If the pattern doesn't provide a schematic (all the patterns in this book do) make a note of the finished measurements and block the knitted pieces accordingly. If you have made any adjustments, such as sleeve length, remember to take this into account.

Once your pieces are pinned out, spray them lightly with water and leave to dry thoroughly. It's amazing how this improves the look of the knitting by evening out any little irregularities in the stitches. It also makes it easier to work with the pieces when putting them together.

TIP: Treat yourself to a blocking board. They come with a grid-marked pad and can be moved about easily.

SEAMING

In most cases, you'll work the seams with the same yarn used for the knitting, but when the yarn is too textured to use easily, choose a smooth matching yarn. Embroidery floss is ideal for this purpose. It comes in a vast range of colors so you'll have no trouble finding a perfect color match. The strands can be separated if you need to use a finer thread. Use a blunt-tipped needle or a large-eye tapestry needle. Pin the seams together with large-head knitter's pins (which don't disappear in the fabric), matching stripes and pattern details, if necessary. Large safety pins also work well, as do various types of clothespins and paper clips. Sets of clips designed for this purpose are available at some knitting suppliers.

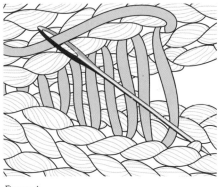

Figure 1

Avoid working with a long length of yarn, because the friction may cause the yarn to break or fray.

Mattress stitch is an excellent, all-purpose seaming stitch that creates an invisible seam. It's worked with the right side of the knitting facing you, making it very easy to match stripes perfectly. To sew a seam in mattress stitch, place the two pieces of knitting to be joined on a flat surface. Thread the needle and work upward one stitch in from the edge, passing the needle under the bar between the first and second rows on one side of the knitting and then moving to the corresponding rows on the other side. Pick up two bars and return to the first piece, going into the knitting at the same point you came out of (see figure 1). Repeat these steps, working from side to side and pulling the seam closed as you go, taking care not to pull so tightly that the knitting is distorted. Your goal is a flat, neat seam. I generally sew from the armhole down to the edge of the sleeve, and from the armhole to the hem, because I find this prevents the seam from drawing up.

Caring for Hand Knits

Most of us want the easiest possible care when it comes to cleaning our clothes, and this is of particular importance where children's knits are concerned. A hand-knitted item is something very special, representing an investment of the knitter's precious time (not to mention money), so the time required to launder a knitted item carefully is really very little compared to the knitting time involved. If you want the garment to be something of an heirloom, you might be inclined to select yarns that require hand washing.

Many of today's washing machines have hand-wash cycles that do the work for you, but by taking just a little more care with knits that are machine-washable, you'll extend the life of the item and make a difference in the way it looks. Don't toss knitwear in with the jeans or towels. Choose a gentle wash cycle with a cool temperature setting, and ensure that wash and rinse cycles are at the same temperature, because sudden changes from hot to cold water will ruin your lovely work. Place the knits in a mesh laundry bag or pillowcase before putting them into the washer. This protects the knitting from harsh spinning, which stretches it out. Resist the impulse to tumble-dry knits even though the care instructions indicate that you can—tumble-drying really does shorten the life of the item. Kids' stuff is small and easy to lay on a laundry rack or large cake rack to dry.

Pity the poor knitter whose generous hand-knitted gift is ruined in the wash. We've all heard these horror stories; so if you're giving your item as a gift, include care instructions in the package. You might package the item in a mesh laundry bag of the appropriate size, tied up with bright ribbon, and then write or print the care instructions on the gift tag. People love to receive a gift wrapped like this, and it's fun to do.

The day will come when the garment is finally outgrown, usually well before it's worn out. If it's to be kept for a younger sibling, or put away with other special childhood memorabilia, launder the item carefully and make any necessary repairs. Knitwear must be completely dry before it's stored. Avoid plastic bags, because the knitting needs to breathe. I use pillowcases to store knitwear; you can pick these up very inexpensively or recycle your worn ones. Tuck a fragrant sachet or something similar inside to keep pesky little munching critters away. Make sure the storage space used is climate-controlled.

Fit to Knit

People who spend long periods of time at the same tasks, such as typing or working on assembly lines, may suffer from repetitive stress injuries (RSI), which can cause great discomfort and disability. It may surprise you to learn that knitting can also cause such an injury, so obviously prevention is far better than cure. Ask any knitter who has developed carpal tunnel syndrome or a frozen shoulder!

It's easy to become so absorbed in your knitting that you spend long periods in the same position, just as a passenger in a car or an airplane might. Here are some general tips to keep you in good knitterly health.

Keep your posture relaxed.

Loosen up!

Avoid gripping the needles.

Try to keep the knitting in your lap.

Don't hold the knitting raised up in front of your face, which puts strain on your shoulders and back.

Hunching up your shoulder to talk on the phone while you knit is an invitation to trouble.

Take regular breaks from your knitting to do some simple stretching exercises.

Swing your arms in a circular motion.

Stretch your arms above your head or out in front of you, with your fingers interlaced.

Wiggle your fingers and wrists.

Raise your shoulders up to your ears and relax again.

Put your arms behind your back and grasp your elbows.

Hug yourself.

You can do many of these simple stretches even while sitting for long periods.

Don't forget to care for your hands, and I'm not referring only to hand cream. Be easy on your hands—use the right tools and implements for the task.

With its perky bows, this refreshingly sweet and simple tank, has ribbon ties that can be adjusted for length, so it grows with the child. Cool and comfortable when worn on its own, it layers well to give a number of wearing options.

EXPERIENCE
LEVEL
Easy

Spring Green Tank

Sizes

3 (4, 6, 8, 10) years

Finished Measurements

Chest: 26 (27, 28, 30, 32)"/
66 (68.5, 71, 96, 81.5)cm

Length: 12 (13, 14, 16, 18)"/
30.5 (33, 35.5, 40.5, 45.5)cm

Materials

Approx total: 235 (282, 315, 375,
440)yd/215 (258, 288, 343,
402)m worsted weight, novelty
cotton-blend yarn

Knitting needles: size 4.5 mm (7
U.S.) and size 5.5 mm (9 U.S.)
or size needed to obtain gauge

Tapestry needle

Crochet hook: size I/ 5.5 mm (9
U.S.)

1¼ yds/1.1 m of ribbon
1"/2.5cm wide

Bodkin

1 skein matching embroidery
floss to use for seaming
(optional)

Gauge

18 sts and 24 rows = 4"/10cm in
rev St st with larger needles

Always take time to check gauge.

Pattern stitch

REV ST ST

Row 1: (RS) P

Row 2: K

Rep rows 1 and 2

Instructions

BACK

Using smaller needles, CO 58 (62,
64, 68, 72) sts. K 5 rows (3 garter st
ridges).

Change to larger needles and rev St
st. Work until piece measures 7½
(8, 8½, 10, 11½)"/19 (20.5, 21.5,
25.5, 29)cm from beg, ending
with a WS row.

Armhole shaping

BO 5 sts at beg of next 2 rows.

Dec 1 st each side every other row,
4 (4, 4, 4, 5) times—40 (44, 46,
50, 52) sts.

Cont until piece measures 10½ (11,
11, 12, 12)"/26.5 (28, 28, 30.5,
30.5)cm from beg, ending with a
WS row.

Neck and shoulder shaping

Work 12 (14, 14, 15, 16) sts, join in a
second ball of yarn, BO 16 (16, 18,
20, 20) sts, then work to end of row.

Working both sides at the same time,
dec 1 st at each neck edge, 2 (2, 2, 3,
3) times.

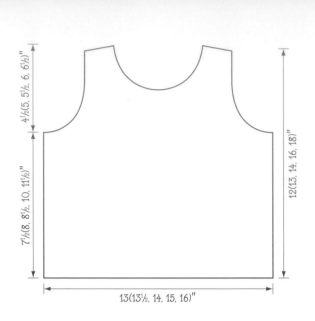

Work until piece measures 12 (13, 14, 16, 18)"/30.5 (33, 35.5, 40.5, 45.5)cm from beg.

Cut yarn, leaving a tail of a few inches. Thread through a tapestry needle, draw up tightly through rem sts, and fasten off.

FRONT
Work same as back.

FINISHING
Sew side seams.

NOTE: You may find it easier to use embroidery floss.

Using crochet hook, work 1 row of single crochet st around neck and armhole edges.

Cut ribbon into 4 pieces of equal length. Thread a bodkin and draw the ribbon ties through shoulders, or pull through with a crochet hook. Tie a saucy bow.

THIS PROJECT WAS MADE WITH:

3 (4, 4, 5, 5) balls of Moda Dea's *Tutu*, 43% nylon/22% cotton/22% acrylic/23% rayon, 1.75oz/50g = 92yd/85m in #3651 (pear green)

Sweet Summer Set

This snappy little jacket is waist length and is knitted in one piece to the armholes. The attractive border details and tiny ruffled sleeves add to its appeal. Stunning buttons are a must! The jacket may be worn over a dress, buttoned as a top, or partnered with the tank peeking out for a really eye-catching outfit. The cute little tank looks adorable worn on its own; the ribbon ties leave room for growth and add to the perky look.

EXPERIENCE
LEVEL
Intermediate

Sizes

3 (4, 6, 8, 10) years

Finished Measurements

Chest: 26 (27, 28, 30, 32)"/66 (68.5, 71, 76, 81.5)cm

Length: 11 (12½, 14, 15 1/2, 17)"/28 (31.5, 35.5, 43)cm

Materials

Approx total: 336 (336, 420, 420, 504)yd/307 (307, 384, 384, 461)m in A and 84yd/77m each in B, C, and D worsted weight yarn

Knitting needles: size 4 mm (6 U.S.) and size 4.5 mm (7 U.S.) *or size needed to obtain gauge*

Circular knitting needle: size 4 mm (6 U.S.), 24"/61cm long

Stitch holders

Stitch markers

Tapestry needle

5 buttons

NOTE: A circular needle will accommodate the stitches more easily, as the jacket is worked in one piece to the underarm, then the work is divided and the back and fronts are worked separately.

Gauge

18 sts and 24 rows = 4"/10cm in St st using larger needles

Always take time to check gauge.

26

Pattern Stitch

Row 1: K

Row 2: K

Row 3: K

Row 4: P

Rep Rows 1–4

Instructions

BODY

NOTES:

Striped border pat is worked over 20 rows.

4 colors are used and each color is worked in 4-row pat st rep.

Carry the yarns not in use loosely along side of work.

Using smaller needles and D, CO 116 (121, 128, 136, 144) sts.

Beg with a p row, work 5 rows in St st.

Change to larger needles.

(RS): Work 4-row pat st rep in following color sequence: B, C, D, A, B.

Cut all colors except A.

Next row (RS): K 2 rows (1 garter st ridge).

Cont working in St st until piece measures 6 (7, 8, 9, 10)"/15 (18, 20.5, 23, 25.5)cm from beg, or to desired length, ending with a WS row.

Divide for fronts and back:

Next row (RS): Work first 29 (30, 32, 34, 36) sts for right front and place rem sts on a holder.

RIGHT FRONT

Armhole and neck shaping

Next row (WS): BO 5 sts at beg of row.

Dec 1 st at neck edge every row, 9 (9, 9, 9, 8) times, then every 2 rows, 1 (2, 4, 5, 6) times; AT THE SAME TIME, dec 1 st at armhole edge every other row, 4 (4, 4, 5, 5) times—10 (10, 10, 10, 12) sts.

Cont until piece measures 11 (12½, 14, 15½, 17)"/28 (31.5, 35.5, 39.5, 43)cm from CO edge.

Place rem 10 (10, 10, 10, 12) shoulder sts on holder.

Place rem 10 (10, 10, 10, 12) sts on each shoulder on separate holders.

BACK

Place next 58 (61, 64, 68, 72) sts on larger needle for back.

BO 5 sts at beg of next 2 rows.

Dec 1 st on each side every other row, 4 (4, 4, 5, 5) times—40 (43, 46, 48, 52) sts.

Cont in St st until back measures 10 (11½, 13, 14½, 16)"/25.5 (29, 33, 37, 40.5)cm from beg, ending with a WS row.

Neck shaping

Next row (RS): Work 11 (11, 11, 11, 13) sts, join in a new ball of yarn, work 18 (21, 24, 26, 26) sts and place on a holder for back neck, work to end of row.

Working both sides at the same time, dec 1 st at each neck edge.

Cont until back measures 11 (12½, 14, 15½, 17)"/28 (31.5, 35.5, 39.5, 43)cm from CO edge.

LEFT FRONT

Next row (RS): Place last 29 (30, 32, 34, 36) sts on larger needle for left front, join in the yarn, BO 5 sts for underarm, and work to end of row.

Complete to match the right front, reversing all shaping.

SLEEVES

Using smaller needles and D, CO 80 (92, 100, 108, 116) sts for ruffle.

Beg with a p row, work 3 rows in St st.

Dec row (RS): *K2tog; rep from * to end of row—40 (46, 50, 54, 58) sts.

Next row: P.

Cut D.

Change to larger needles. Join in C and k 2 rows (1 garter st ridge).

Work 5 rows in St st.

Next row (WS): K.

Cut D.

Join in A and work in St st until piece measures 2½ (2½, 3, 3, 3)"/6.5 (6.5, 7.5, 7.5, 7.5)cm, ending with a WS row.

Cap shaping

BO 5 sts at beg of next 2 rows.

Dec 1 st at each side every other row, 4 (4, 4, 4, 5) times.

Dec 1 st at each side every row, 3 (5, 7, 9, 9) times.

BO 1 (1, 2, 2, 2) sts at beg of next 4 rows.

BO rem 12 (14, 10, 10, 12) sts.

FINISHING

Block pieces by spraying lightly with water.

Place each set of shoulder sts on separate needles and work a 3-needle BO.

FRONT BANDS

Mark position of buttons on left front, placing first one ½"/1 cm below beg of neck shaping and last one ½"/1cm from bottom edge, with rem buttons spaced evenly between.

With RS facing, using 24"/61cm circular needle, beg with first pat st row on right bottom edge, pick up and k29 (32, 36, 42, 46) sts to beg of neck shaping, 20 (24, 25, 30, 30) sts along right neck edge, 18 (21, 24, 26, 26) sts from back holder, 20 (24, 25, 30, 30) sts along left neck edge, and 29 (32, 36, 42, 46) sts along left front—116 (133, 146, 170, 178) sts.

K 3 rows.

Next row: K and work buttonholes
(k2tog, yo) to correspond with
button markers.

K 4 rows.

BO loosely.

Sew sleeve seams.

Pin sleeves into armholes and sew in
place.

Sew on buttons.

Darn in loose ends.

TANK

Sizes

3 (4, 6, 8, 10) years

Finished Measurements

Chest: 24 (25, 26, 28, 30)"/61
(63.5, 66, 71, 76)cm

Length: 9 (10, 12, 13, 15)"/23
(25.5, 30.5, 33, 38)cm

Materials

Approx total: 252 (252, 336, 336,
420)yd/230 (230, 307, 307,
384)m in A and 84yd/77m
each in B and C worsted
weight yarn

Knitting needles: size 4.25 mm
(6 U.S.) and size 4.5.mm
(7 U.S) *or size needed to
obtain gauge*

Crochet hook: 4 mm (G/6 U.S.)

1¼yd/1.1m of ribbon,
⅜"/1.5cm wide

Tapestry needle

Gauge

18 sts and 24 rows = 4"/10cm in
St st using larger needles

Always take time to check gauge.

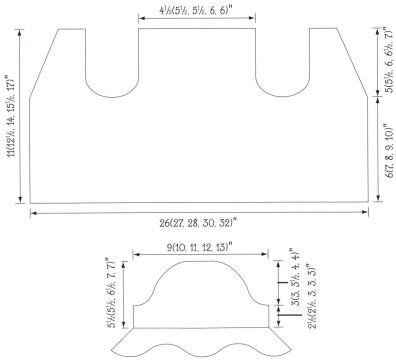

Instructions

BACK

Using smaller needles and B, CO 108 (112, 120, 128, 136) sts for ruffle.

Beg with a p row, work 3 rows in St st.

Dec row (RS): *K2tog; rep from * to end of row—54 (56, 60, 64, 68) sts.

Next row: P.

Cut B.

Change to larger needles. Join in C and k 2 rows (1 garter st ridge).

Work 5 rows in St st.

Next row (WS): K.

Cut C.

Join in A and work in St st until piece measures 6 (7, 8, 9, 10)"/15 (18, 20.5, 23, 25.5)cm, or to desired length, ending with a WS row.

Armhole shaping

BO 4 (4, 4, 5, 5) sts at beg of next 2 rows.

Dec 1 st each side every other row, 3 (3, 3, 4, 4) times—40 (42, 46, 46, 50) sts.

Cont until piece measures 3 (3, 4, 4, 5)"/7.5 (7.5, 10, 10, 12.5)cm from beg of armhole shaping, ending with a RS row.

Foldline for ribbon casing

Next row (WS): K.

Work 3 more rows in St st.

BO sts.

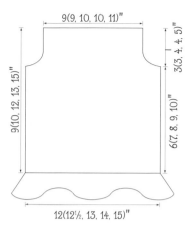

FRONT

Work as for back until piece measures 2 (2, 3, 3, 4)"/5 (5, 7.5, 7.5, 10)cm from beg of armhole shaping, ending with a RS row.

Complete ribbon casing as for back.

FINISHING

Block pieces and spray lightly with water.

Sew side seams.

Fold casing to inside along foldline and stitch in place.

Using A and crochet hook, work 1 row single crochet st around armhole edges.

Darn in loose ends.

Cut ribbon to desired length and thread through casing on front and back.

Adjust the fit and tie bows.

THIS PROJECT WAS MADE WITH:

3 (3, 4, 4, 5) balls of Sweater Kits' *CottonLicious*, 100% cotton, 1.75oz/50g = 84yd/77m in #2 (hot pink) (A) and 1 ball each in #4 (spring green) (B) and #5 (ocean) (C)

The exposed seam and piping details of this crisply styled sweater look great in all types of yarn. Choose a strong color contrast for maximum impact, and this easy-fit piece is sure to become a seasonal favorite.

Top of the Class Sweater

Sizes

3 (4, 6, 8, 10, 12) years

Finished Measurements

Chest: 26 (27, 28, 30, 32, 34)"/66 (68.5, 71, 76, 81.5, 86.5)cm

Length: 13 (14½, 15½, 17½, 19½, 21)"/33 (37, 39.5, 44.5, 49.5, 53.5)cm

Materials

Approx total: 355 (450, 510, 620, 730, 840)yd/233 (411, 466, 567, 667, 768)m in A; 45 (45, 50, 50, 50, 50)yd/41 (41, 46, 46, 46, 46)m in B worsted weight yarn

Knitting needles: size 4mm (6 U.S) and size 5mm (8 U.S.) *or size needed to obtain gauge*

Circular knitting needles (cn): 5 mm (8 U.S.), 16"/40cm long

Stitch markers

Stitch holders

Tapestry needle

Gauge

18 sts and 24 rows = 4"/10cm in St st using larger needles

Always take time to check gauge.

Instructions

BACK

With smaller needles and B, CO 56 (58, 62, 66, 70, 74) sts. Work 1 row in k1, p1 rib.

Cut yarn, join in A. Cont in rib for 1½ (2, 2, 2, 2, 2)"/4 (5, 5, 5, 5, 5) cm.

Next row (RS): K2, inc 1 st, work to last 3 sts, inc 1 st, work to end—58 (60, 64, 68, 72, 76) sts.

Change to larger needles. Work in St st until piece measures 7½ (8½, 9, 10½, 12, 13)"/19 (21.5, 23, 26.5, 30.5, 33)cm.

Place markers for underarm seams.

Cont until piece measures 12½ (14, 15, 17, 19, 20½)"/31.5 (35.5, 38, 43, 48.5, 52)cm from CO edge, ending with a WS row.

Next row (RS): K20 (19, 20, 21, 23, 25) sts, place center 18 (22, 24, 26, 26, 26) sts on a holder, attach another ball of yarn, k to end of row.

Working both sides at the same time, dec 1 st at each neck edge on next row.

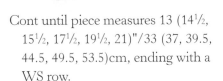

other row, 5 (6, 6, 7, 7, 7) times—
19 (18, 19, 20, 22, 24) sts each
side.

Cont until piece measures 13 (14½,
15½, 17½, 19½, 21)"/33 (37, 39.5,
44.5, 49.5, 53.5)cm, ending with a
WS row.

Work shoulder sts in contrast yarn
as for back.

SLEEVES

With smaller needles and B, CO
30 (32, 34, 36, 38, 38) sts. Work 1
row in k1, p1 rib.

Cut yarn, join A, and cont in rib for
1½ (2, 2, 2, 2, 2)"/4 (5, 5, 5, 5,
5)cm.

Change to larger needles and St st.

Sleeve Shaping

Inc 1 st on each side every 3rd (4th,
4th, 4th, 4th, 4th) row until there
are 50 (54, 58, 64, 68, 72) sts.

Work until sleeve measures 7½ (10,
11, 12½, 14, 15)"/19 (25.5, 28,
31.5, 35.5, 38)cm from beg, ending with a WS row.

With RS facing, cut A, join B, and k
1 row.

Leave all sts on holder.

FINISHING

Block pieces to measurements.

Join shoulders

Place back and front pieces together
at one of the shoulder seams with
WS facing, so that RS is facing
you. Slip sts from holders onto

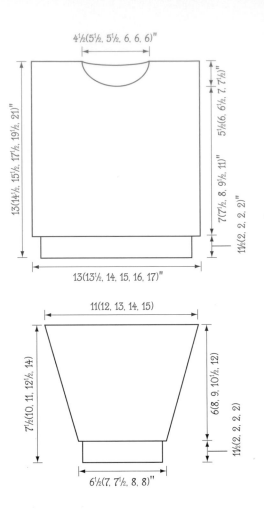

larger needles. With a third needle
and contrasting color yarn, BO
sts, thus creating the exposed
seam.

Complete second shoulder in the
same way.

Neck

With RS facing, using circular needle and A, pick up and k approx
58 (64, 68, 74, 76, 78) sts around
neck edge, including sts on holders. (See page 13.) Adjust sts, if
necessary, to ensure an even number. Join and work around in k1,
p1 rib for 1"/2.5cm.

Cont until piece measures 13 (14½,
15½, 17½, 19½, 21)"/33 (37, 39.5,
44.5, 49.5, 53.5)cm, ending with a
WS row.

With RS facing, cut A, join B, and k
1 row on 19 (18, 19, 20, 22, 24) sts
of each shoulder.

Leave shoulder sts on separate
holders.

FRONT

Work as for back until piece measures 10 (11, 12, 14, 16, 17)"/25.5
(28, 30.5, 35.5, 40.5, 43)cm from
beg, ending with a WS row.

Neck Shaping

Next row (RS): K24 (24, 25, 27, 29,
31) sts, place center 10 (12, 14, 14,
14, 14) sts on a holder, attach another ball of yarn, k to end of row.

Working both sides at the same time,
dec 1 st at each neck edge every

Cut A, join B, and work 1 more row in rib.

BO loosely in rib.

Armhole Seams

With RS facing, using larger needles and B, pick up and k50 (54, 58, 64, 68, 72) sts between markers, taking care to have an equal number of sts on each side of shoulder seam.

Place sts of first sleeve onto second larger needle and work a 3-needle BO as you did for the shoulder seams.

Rep for second sleeve.

Join body sleeve seams neatly.

Weave in all ends.

THIS PROJECT WAS MADE WITH:

2 (3, 3, 4, 4, 5) balls of Bernat's *Denimstyle*, 70% acrylic/30% soft cotton, 3.5oz/100g = 196yd/179m in #03108 (indigo) (A)

1 ball of Plymouth's *Encore Worsted Weight*, 75% acrylic/25% wool, 3.5oz/100g = 150yd/137m in #1386 (B)

air it with a gypsy skirt, jeans, or cropped pants—this versatile vest looks delightful in any setting. It's knitted in one piece to the underarm, while the neat hemline and crochet-edge finish keep the styling classically simple. It's also great fun to knit!

Sizes

3 (4, 6, 8, 10) years

Finished Measurements

Chest: 26 (27, 29, 30, 32)"/
66 (68.5, 73.5, 76, 81.5)cm

Length: 13 (14½, 15½, 17½, 19½)"/
33 (37, 39.5, 44.5, 49.5)cm

Materials

Approx total: 197yd/180m each
in A and B worsted weight
yarn and 46 (46, 92, 92, 92)yd/
42 (42, 84, 84, 84)m in C novelty yarn

Knitting needles: size 4 mm (6
U.S.) and size 5 mm (8 U.S.) or
size needed to obtain gauge

Stitch holders

Crochet hook: size H/5 mm (8
U.S.)

Tapestry needle

Ribbon or cord of your choice
for the ties

Beads (optional)

NOTE: A circular knitting needle
24"/61cm will hold the stitches
more easily, but is not essential.

Gauge

18 sts and 24 rows = 4"/10cm in
St st using worsted-weight yarn
and larger needles

Always take time to check gauge.

Carnival Vest

Pattern Stitch

(16-row repeat)

Rows 1–5: With A, beg on RS with a
k row, work in St st

Row 6 (WS): With A, k

Row 7: With B, k

Row 8: With B, p

Rows 9–10: With A, k

Rows 11–15: With B,
work in St st

Row 16 (WS): With C, k

Instructions

BODY

With smaller needles and A, CO
116 (122, 128, 136, 144) sts. Work
in St st for 1"/2.5cm, ending with
a RS row.

Next row (WS): K to form foldline
for hem.

Change to larger needles. Work in
pat st until piece measures 8½
(9½, 10, 11½, 13)"/21.5 (24, 25.5,
29, 33)cm from beg, carrying the
yarns not in use loosely along side
of work, ending with a WS row.

Divide for fronts and back:

Next row (RS): Work 24 (25, 27, 29,
31) sts for right front, BO 10 sts

for underarm, work until 48 (52, 54, 58, 62) sts rem for back, BO 10 sts for second underarm, work rem 24 (25, 27, 29, 31) sts for left front.

LEFT FRONT

Next row (WS): Work 24 (25, 27, 29, 31) sts for left front and place rem sts on a holder.

Dec 1 st at armhole edge on next and every other row, 3 (3, 3, 3, 4) times more—20 (21, 23, 25, 26) sts.

Cont in pat until piece measures 11½ (13, 14, 15½, 17½)"/29 (33, 35.5, 39.5, 44.5)cm from beg, ending with a RS row.

Neck Shaping

BO 7 (9, 9, 9, 9) sts at neck edge once.

BO 2 sts at neck edge once.

Dec 1 st at neck edge every other row, 1 (1, 2, 3, 3) times.

Cont working in pat until the piece measures 14 (15½, 16½, 18½, 20½)"/35.5 (39.5, 42, 47, 52)cm.

BO rem 10 (9, 10, 11, 12) shoulder sts.

RIGHT FRONT

Place right front sts from holder onto needle.

With WS facing, join in yarn at underarm and work to match left front, reversing all shaping.

BACK

Place back sts from holder onto needle.

With WS facing, join in yarn and keeping the pat correct, dec 1 st at each armhole edge on next row

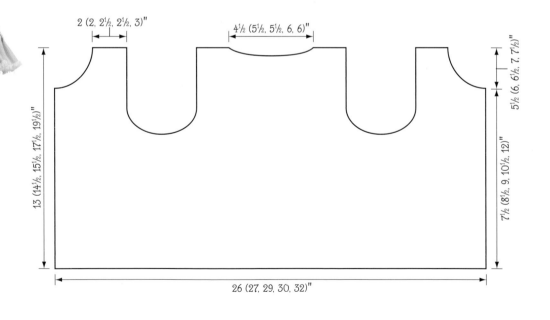

2 (2, 2½, 2½, 3)"

4½ (5½, 5½, 6, 6)"

5½ (6, 6½, 7, 7½)"

13 (14½, 15½, 17½, 19½)"

7½ (8½, 9, 10½, 12)"

26 (27, 29, 30, 32)"

and every other row, 3 (3, 3, 3, 4) times more—40 (44, 46, 50, 52) sts. Cont until piece measures 13 (14½, 15½, 17½, 19½)"/33 (37, 39.5, 44.5, 49.5)cm from beg, ending with a WS row.

Neck Shaping

Next row (RS): Work 11 (10, 11, 12, 13) sts, join in a second ball of yarn, BO 18 (24, 24, 26, 26) sts, k to end of row.

Working both sides at the same time, dec 1 st at each neck edge once.

Work until piece measures 14 (15½, 16½, 18½, 20½)"/35.5 (39.5, 42, 47, 52)cm from beg.

BO rem 10 (9, 10, 11, 12) sts on each shoulder.

FINISHING

Spray very lightly with water.

Turn up hem at foldline and stitch in place.

Seam shoulders.

Edging

With crochet hook and A, work 1 row single crochet around arm-holes.

Starting at hem edge, work 1 row single crochet around front and neck edges.

Front Ties

Cut 2 lengths of ribbon or cord and attach at neck edges.

Thread beads (if using) and tie knots at the ends of the cords to secure them.

NOTE: A button and loop, or a decorative pin, may be used for the closure, if preferred.

TIP: Use a tapestry needle or crochet hook to pull the "tails" of novelty yarn out for the best effect.

THIS PROJECT WAS MADE WITH:

1 ball each of Lion Brand's *Wool-Ease Worsted Weight*, 80% acrylic/20% wool, 3oz/85g = 197yd/180m in #117 (colonial blue) (A) and #148 (turquoise) (B)

1 (1, 2, 2, 2) balls of Lion Brand's *Fun Fetti*, 89% polyester/11% nylon, 1.75oz/50g = 46yd/42m in #206 (beach party blue) (C)

W arm enough to stand up to a salty sea breeze and oversized for comfortable layering, this sweater features a tailored edging that doesn't pull in, as well as a practical buttoned-tab neckline. The sleeves are knitted from the top down, making it simple to adjust the length. It's stylish and comfortable—a sweater a kid can live in throughout the winter months.

EXPERIENCE
LEVEL
. . . .
Intermediate

Sea Captain Sweater

Sizes

3 (4, 6, 8, 10) years

Finished Measurements

Chest: 31 (32, 34, 35, 37)"/79 (81.5, 86.5, 89)cm

Length: 14 (15½, 16½, 18½, 20½)"/35.5 (39.5, 42, 47, 52)cm

Materials

Approx total: 372 (372, 372, 496, 620)yd/340 (340, 340, 453, 567)m bulky weight yarn

Knitting needles: size 6 mm (10 U.S.) and size 8 mm (11 U.S.) *or size needed to obtain gauge*

Stitch holders

Stitch markers

Tapestry needle

3 buttons

Gauge

10 sts and 16 rows = 4"/10cm in St st using larger needles

Always take time to check gauge.

Pattern Stitch

BROKEN RIB

Row 1: K

Row 2: K1, p1 across

Rep Rows 1–2

Instructions

BACK

Using smaller needles, CO 38 (40, 42, 44, 46) sts. Beg with Row 2 of pat st, work in broken rib pat for 2½ (3, 3, 3, 3)"/6.5 (7.5, 7.5, 7.5, 7.5)cm. Note: CO row counts as Row 1.

Change to larger needles. Work in St st until piece measures 14 (15½, 16½, 18½, 20½)"/35.5 (39.5, 42, 47, 52)cm from beg.

Place 14 (13, 14, 14, 15) sts at each end on separate holders for shoulders and center 10 (14, 14, 16, 16) sts on a holder for back neck.

FRONT

Work as for back until piece measures 10½ (11½, 12, 14, 15½)"/26.5 (29, 30.5, 35.5, 39.5)cm from beg, ending with a WS row.

Placket Shaping

Next row: Work 17 (18, 19, 20, 21) sts, join in another ball of yarn, BO center 4 sts, work to end of row.

Working both sides at the same time, cont for 2½ (3, 3, 3, 3½)"/6.5 (7.5, 7.5, 7.5, 9)cm more.

Neck Shaping

Place 2 (4, 3, 4, 4) sts at each neck edge on separate holders.

Dec 1 st at each neck edge every other row, 1 (1, 2, 2, 2) times.

Cont until front measures same as back to shoulder.

Leave rem 14 (13, 14, 14, 15) sts on each shoulder on separate holders.

SLEEVES

Place shoulder sts on separate needles and join using 3-needle BO.

Place markers 5½ (6, 6½, 7, 7½)"/ 14 (15, 16.5, 18, 19)cm down from each shoulder seam on front and back.

With RS facing, using larger needles, pick up and k28 (30, 32, 36, 38) sts between markers, dividing sts equally on each side of shoulder seam.

Sleeve Shaping

Size 3 only: Dec 1 st on each side every 4th row 4 times, then every 2nd row, 2 times.

Sizes 4 (6, 8, 10): Dec 1 st on each side every 6th row, 2 (4, 3, 6) times, then every 4th row, 4 (2, 5, 2) times.

All sizes: There will be 16 (18, 20, 20, 22) sts on needles.

Cont working until sleeve measures 6 (8, 9, 10½, 12)"/15 (20.5, 23, 26.5, 30.5)cm.

Change to smaller needles. Work in pat st for 1½ (2, 2, 2, 2)"/4 (5, 5, 5, 5)cm.

BO loosely in rib.

FINISHING

Block pieces to measurements.

Neckband

With RS facing, using smaller needles and beg at right front, k2 (4, 3, 4, 4) from holder, pick up and k5 (5, 6, 6, 7) sts along the right neck edge, k10 (14, 14, 16, 16) back neck sts rem on holder, pick up and k5 (5, 6, 6, 7) sts along left neck edge, k2 (4, 3, 4, 4) sts from holder—24 (32, 32, 36, 38) sts.

Work in pat st for 1"/2.5cm.

BO loosely in rib.

Right Placket

With RS facing, using smaller needles, pick up and k10 (12, 14, 14, 16) sts along right placket edge.

Work in pat st for 1"/2.5cm.

BO loosely in rib.

Mark position of 3 buttons evenly spaced on placket.

Left Placket

With RS facing, using smaller needles, pick up and k10 (12, 14, 14, 16) sts along left placket edge.

Work in pat st for 1"/2.5cm, working buttonholes (k2tog, yo) after ½"/1cm to correspond with position of buttons.

BO loosely in rib.

Sew overlap neatly in place.

Position underlap on inside and sew.

Sew side and sleeve seams.

Sew on buttons.

Darn in loose ends.

THIS PROJECT WAS MADE WITH:

3 (3, 3, 4, 5) balls of Reynold's *Smile*, 72% acrylic/28% wool, 3.5oz/100g = 124yds/113m in #106

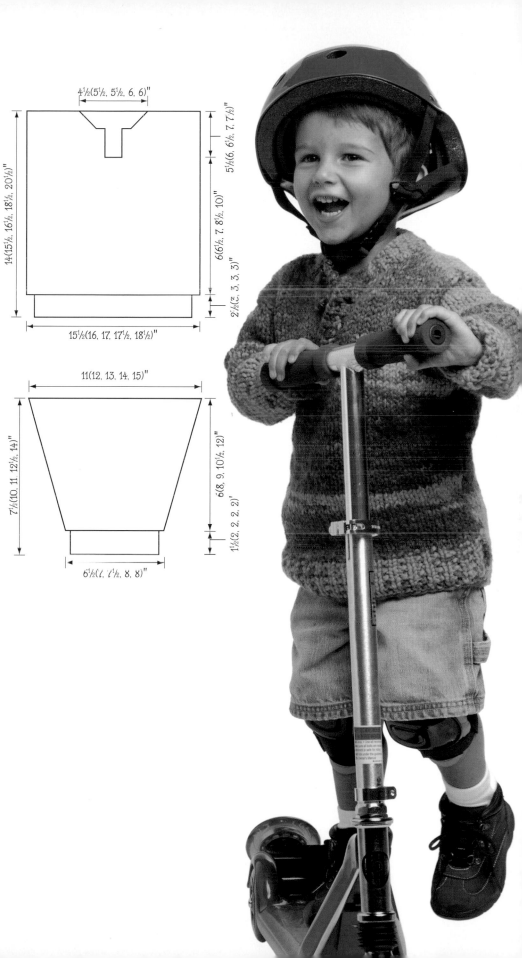

4½(5½, 5½, 6, 6)"

5½(6, 6½, 7, 7½)"

14(15½, 16½, 18½, 20½)"

6(6½, 7, 8½, 10)"

2½(2, 3, 3, 3)"

15½(16, 17, 17½, 18½)"

11(12, 13, 14, 15)"

7½(10, 11, 12½, 14)"

6(8, 9, 10½, 12)"

1½(2, 2, 2, 2)"

6½(7, 7½, 8, 8)"

Designed to be worn over a shirt or tee, this practical sweater in a two-color seed stitch pattern allows room for growth, while the side vents provide wearing ease for active kids. The sleeves are knitted from the top down and, because the fabric is fully reversible, can be made longer and cuffed back, thus extending the life of the garment.

EXPERIENCE
LEVEL
·················
Intermediate

Girl on the Go Sweater and Hat Set

Sizes

3 (4, 6, 8, 10) years

Finished Measurements

Chest: 26 (27, 28, 30, 32)"/66 (68.5, 71, 76, 81.5)cm

Length: 15 (16½, 17½, 19½, 21½"/ 38 (40.5, 44.5, 49.5, 54.5)cm

Materials

Approx total: 306 (306, 306, 459, 459)yd/280 (280, 280, 420, 420)m in A and 306yd/280m in B chunky weight yarn

Knitting needles: size 6.5 mm (10½ U.S.) or size needed to obtain gauge

Circular knitting needle: size 6.5 mm (10½ U.S.), 24"/61cm long

Set double-pointed needles: size 6.5 mm (10½ U.S.) (for hat)

Stitch markers

Stitch holders

Tapestry needle

Gauge

14 sts and 18 rows/rnds = 4"/10cm in St st

Always take time to check gauge.

SWEATER

Pattern Stitch

TWO-COLOR SEED STITCH
(worked back and forth over an odd number of sts)

Rows 1–2: *With A, k1, p1; rep from * to last st, k1

Rows 3–4: With B, rep Rows 1–2

Rep Rows 1–4 for pat st, always having a k st over a p st and a p st over a k st

TWO-COLOR SEED STITCH
(worked in-the-rnd over an odd number of sts)

Rnd 1: *With A, k1, p1; rep from * around to last st, k1.

Rnd 2: *With A, p1, k1; rep from * around to last st, p1.

Rnds 3–4: With B, rep Rnds 1 and 2.

Rep Rnds 1–4 for pat st, always having a k st over a p st and a p st over a k st.

Instructions

BACK

NOTE: Do not cut and join in yarns, but carry loosely along at the edge of the knitting.

With B, CO 45 (47, 51, 53, 57) sts. Work back and forth in pat st for 9½ (10½, 11, 12½, 14)"/24 (26.5, 28, 31.5, 35.5)cm. Place markers for underarm.

Cont until piece measures 13 (14½, 15½, 17½, 19½)"/33 (37, 39.5, 44.5, 49.5)cm from CO edge, ending with a WS row.

Neck Shaping

Next row (RS): Work 16 (16, 17, 17, 18) sts, work next 15 (17, 18, 20, 20) sts for back neck and place them on a holder, join another ball of yarn, and work to end of row.

Working both sides at the same time, dec 1 st at each neck edge once.

Cont until piece measures 15 (16½, 17½, 19½, 21½)"/38 (42, 44.5, 49.5, 54.5)cm from beg.

Leave rem 15 (15, 16, 16, 17) sts on each shoulder on separate holders.

FRONT

Work as for back until piece measures 12 (13½, 14½, 16½, 18½)"/30.5 (34.5, 37, 42, 47)cm from beg, ending with a WS row.

Neck Shaping

Next row (RS): Work 18 (18, 20, 20, 22) sts, work next 9 (11, 11, 13, 13) sts for front neck and place them on a holder, join another ball of yarn, and work to end of row.

Working both sides at the same time, dec 1 st at each neck edge every other row, 3 (3, 4, 4, 4) times. Cont in pat until piece measures the same as the back.

Leave rem 15 (15, 16, 16, 17) sts on each shoulder on separate holders.

SLEEVES

TIP: Pick up sleeve sts with same color on each side and BO with same color so that sleeves match.

Place shoulder sts on separate needles and join using a 3-needle BO.

With RS facing, using B, pick up and k39 (43, 47, 51, 53) sts evenly between underarm markers.

Work back and forth in pat st for 1 row.

Sleeve Shaping

Maintaining pat as decs are worked, dec 1 st on each side every other row, 2 (2, 2, 0, 0) times, then every 4 rows, 5 (7, 8, 11, 11) times—25 (25, 27, 29, 31) sts.

Cont in pat until sleeve measures 7½ (10, 11, 12, 13)"/19 (25.5, 28, 30.5, 33)cm or desired length.

BO loosely.

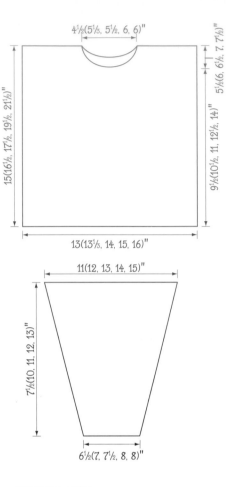

NECKBAND

With RS facing, using circular needle and B, pick up and k approx 46 (50, 54, 60, 64) sts around neck opening, including sts on holders.

BO loosely.

FINISHING

Sew side seams, leaving last 4"/10cm open for side vents.

Sew sleeve seams.

Darn in any loose ends.

HAT

Instructions

Using circular needles and B, CO 57
(65) sts. Join, taking care not to
twist sts. Place marker and work
around in pat st for 4 (5)"/10
(12.5) cm. Cut B.

Next rnd: With A, inc 1 st in first st
and continue working around in St
st (k every rnd) on 58 (66) sts until
piece measures 7 (8)"/18 (20.5)cm
from CO edge.

Next rnd: K2tog around 29 (33)
sts.

NOTE: Change to dpns when necessary.

Next rnd: *K2tog; rep from * to
last st, k 1—15 (17) sts.

Cut yarn and thread through a
tapestry needle. Draw up rem
sts tightly and fasten off.

Darn in loose ends.

THESE PROJECTS WERE MADE WITH:

2 (2, 2, 3, 3) balls of Lion Brand's
Wool-Ease Chunky, 80%
acrylic/20% wool, 5oz/140g =
153yds/140m in #140 (deep rose)
(A) and 2 balls in #146 (orchid) (B)

Knitting this vest is great fun, as only two colors are used in the design, and the variegated yarn makes the stitch pattern look more intricate than it really is. The corrugated ribbing adds to the traditional look. The vest is knitted in the round to the armhole, then the work is divided and the back and front are worked separately. If you've never tried Fair Isle knitting before, don't be afraid to tackle this—you'll be amazed at how quickly you'll get it!

EXPERIENCE
LEVEL
....
Experienced

Fair Isle Vest

Sizes

3 (4, 6, 8, 10) years

Finished Measurements

Chest. 26 (27, 28, 30, 32)"/66 (68.5, 71, 76, 81.5)cm

Length: 13 (14 1/2, 15 1/2, 17 1/2, 19 1/2)"/33 (37, 39.5, 44.5, 49.5)cm

Materials

Approx total: 200 (200, 200, 200, 400)yd/183 (183, 183, 183, 366)m each of A and B worsted weight yarn

Circular knitting needles: size 5 mm (8 U.S.) and size 5.5 mm (9 U.S.), 24"/61cm long, or size needed to obtain gauge

Circular knitting needle (or set of double-pointed needles): size 5 mm (8 U.S.), 16"/40cm long

Stitch holders

Stitch markers

Tapestry needle

Gauge

18 sts and 24 rows = 4"/10cm in St st using larger needles

Always take time to check gauge

Pattern Stitches

NOTES:

Long-tail cast on gives a nice edge to the corrugated ribbing.

All rounds will be in knit stitch when working the Fair Isle pattern in the round. After the knitting is divided for the front and back, it will be worked back and forth in rows in St st (k 1 row, p 1 row).

Strand the yarn not in use loosely across the back of the knitting.

Working with a color in each hand makes it much easier to knit Fair Isle, so make it a point to learn this technique if you don't already know how.

CORRUGATED RIBBING

All rnds: *K2B, p2A, repeat from * around.

FAIR ISLE PATTERN

Rnds 1–2: K

Rnds 3–4: *K2A, k2B; rep from * to end of rnd

Rnds 5–6: *K2B, k2A; rep from * to end of rnd

Rnds 7–8: *K2A, k2B; rep from * to end of rnd

Rep Rnds 1–8

Instructions

BODY

Using smaller needles and A, CO 116 (124, 128, 136, 144) sts. Join into a rnd, being careful not to twist sts.

Place a marker for beg of rnd, join in B, and work corrugated ribbing for 1½ (2, 2, 2, 2)"/4 (5, 5, 5, 5)cm.

With A, k 1 rnd.

P 1 rnd.

Change to larger needles. Work in Fair Isle pat until piece measures 7½ (8½, 9, 10½, 12)"/19 (21.5, 23, 26.5, 30.5)cm from beg.

BACK

Armhole Shaping

Next row (RS): BO 4 sts at beg of rnd, work 54 (58, 60, 64, 68) sts, slip rem sts onto a holder, and turn work.

Next row (WS): BO 4 sts at beg of row, p to end of row, keeping pat correct—50 (54, 56, 60, 64) sts.

Work back and forth in St st until piece measures 13 (14½, 15½, 17½, 19½)"/33 (37, 39.5, 44.5, 49.5)cm from beg.

Place 16 (16, 16, 17, 19) sts at each end onto separate holders for shoulders.

Place center 18 (22, 24, 26, 26) sts onto a holder for back neck.

FRONT

Slip front sts onto needle.

Armhole Shaping

Next row (RS): BO 4 sts, work 25 (27, 28, 30, 32) sts, join in another ball of yarn, and work to end of row.

Next row (WS): BO 4 sts at beg of row, p to end of row, keeping pat correct.

Work both sides of front at the same time, working back and forth in St st and keeping the pat correct.

Neck Shaping

Dec 1 st at each neck edge every 2 rows, 7 (9, 10, 10, 9) times, then every 4 rows, 2 (2, 2, 3, 4) times.

Work in pat until piece measures same as back to shoulder.

Place 16 (16, 16, 17, 19) shoulder sts onto separate holders.

FINISHING

Block pieces to measurements.

With each set of shoulder sts on separate needles, work a 3-needle BO.

Neckband

Beg at center front, using smaller needle and A, pick up and k29 (31, 34, 36, 38) sts along right neck edge, k18 (22, 24, 26, 26) back neck sts from holder, pick up and k29 (31, 34, 36, 38) sts along right neck edge—76 (84, 92, 100, 108) sts.

Adjust number of sts by inc or dec so that total number is divisible by 4.

Turn work and k 1 row in A.

Work corrugated rib, back and forth in rows, for 1"/2.5cm.

Using A, BO loosely in rib.

Sleeve Bands

Beg at underarm, using 16"/40cm long circular needle and A, pick up and k56 (60, 68, 76, 80) sts around armhole edge.

Adjust number of sts by inc or dec so that total number is divisible by 4.

P 1 row in A.

Work corrugated rib in rnds for 1"/2.5cm.

Using A, BO loosely in rib.

Lap ends of neckband and stitch neatly in place.

Darn in loose ends.

4½(5½, 5½, 6, 6)"

13(14½, 15½, 17½, 19½)"

5½(6, 6½, 7, 7½)"

6(6½, 7, 8½, 10)"

1½(2, 2, 2, 2)"

13(13½, 14, 15, 16)"

Stranded Knitting

Working small patterns with
more than one color in a row
has increasingly come to be
known as Fair Isle knitting,
after this tiny island north of
Scotland. Traditional Fair Isle
knitting is worked in the
round using only two colors
in each row, with the yarns
being carried across the back
of the work. This can cause
the knitting to pucker, so it's
important to keep an even
tension as you knit. Get into
the habit of spreading your
knitting out along the needle
to ensure that it remains elastic; don't bunch the stitches
up close together. You can
hold the yarns in the same
hand, but it's easier if you're
able to work with one color in
each hand. To do this, you'll
need to know both the
English and the Continental
knitting methods, if you don't
already. It's well worth taking
the trouble to learn them if
this kind of color work
appeals to you. There are
many excellent books on the
subject. Fair warning—this
kind of knitting can be great
fun and very addictive!

This sweet cotton top features three-quarter-length sleeves which are knitted from the top down and a ribbon-tied neckline. The embellishment details are optional, but a few beads and a pretty button or two will really make this top special. If embellishment is your thing, you can showcase your skills here, or you may prefer to knit the top in a variegated yarn and omit the detailing. Either version looks good and offers many options for three-season wear.

EXPERIENCE
LEVEL
••••••••••••••••
Intermediate

Gypsy Top

Sizes

3 (4, 6, 8, 10) years

Finished Measurements

Chest: 26 (27, 28, 30, 32)"/66 (68.5, 71, 76, 81.5)cm

Length: 13 (14½, 15½, 17½, 19½)"/33 (37, 39.5, 44.5, 49.5)cm

Sleeve length: 6 (7½, 8, 9, 10½)"/ 15 (19, 20, 23, 26.5)cm

Materials

Approx total: 450 (450, 600, 600, 750)yd/411 (411, 548, 548, 686)m worsted weight yarn

Knitting needles: size 4 mm (6 U.S.) and size 4.5 mm (7 U.S.) or size needed to obtain gauge

Stitch markers

Stitch holders

Crochet hook: size 4.5 mm (7 U.S.)

Embellishments: embroidery floss, small buttons, beads (optional)

Tapestry needle

Bodkin

Ribbon or cord for ties

Gauge

20 sts and 26 rows = 4"/10cm in St st using larger needles

Always take time to check gauge.

Instructions

BACK

Using smaller needles, CO 66 (68, 72, 76, 80) sts. Work in k1, p1 rib for 1"/2.5cm

Change to larger needles and St st. Work until piece measures 7½ (8½, 9, 10½, 12) "/19 (21.5, 23, 26.5, 30.5)cm from beg.

Place markers for underarm.

Cont until piece measures 11½ (13, 14, 15½, 17½)"/29 (33, 35.5, 39.5, 44.5)cm from beg, ending with a WS row.

Neck Shaping

Next row (RS): K23 (24, 25, 26, 28) sts, join in a second ball of yarn, BO 20 (20, 22, 24, 24) sts, k to end of row.

Working both sides at the same time, work 1 row, then dec 1 st at each neck edge every other row, 4 (4, 4, 4, 6) times.

Cont until piece measures 13 (14½, 15½, 17½, 19½)"/33 (37, 39.5, 44.5, 49.5)cm from beg.

Leave rem 19 (20, 21, 22, 22) sts on each side on separate holders for shoulders.

FRONT

Work as for back until front measures 8½ (9½, 10, 11½, 13)"/21.5 (24, 25.5, 29, 33)cm from beg, ending with a WS row.

Next row (RS): K33 (34, 36, 38, 40) sts and place rem sts on a holder.

LEFT FRONT

Continue working on left front sts until piece measures 10 (11, 11½, 13½, 15)"/25.5 (28, 29, 34.5, 38)cm from CO edge, ending with a RS row.

Neck Shaping

Next row (WS): BO 11 (11, 12, 12, 13) sts at neck edge, work to end of row.

Dec 1 st at neck edge every other row, 3 (3, 3, 4, 5) times.

Cont until piece measures same as back to shoulder.

Leave rem 19 (20, 21, 22, 23) shoulder sts on a holder.

RIGHT FRONT

Return to sts on holder and place them on needle. Join yarn and work to match left front, reversing shaping.

SLEEVES

Place shoulder sts on separate needles and work a 3-needle BO.

With RS facing and using larger needles, pick up and k56 (60, 66, 70, 76) sts between markers.

NOTE: Take care to pick up an equal number of sts on each side of shoulder seam.

Dec 1 st on each side every 4 (4, 4, 5, 5) rows until 44 (46, 48, 50, 56) sts rem.

Work straight until sleeve measures 5 (6½, 7, 8, 9½)"/12.5 (16.5, 18, 20.5, 24)cm.

Adjust sleeve length here, if desired.

Change to smaller needles. Work in k1, p1 rib for 1"/2.5cm.

BO in rib.

FINISHING

Pin knitted pieces out and spray lightly with water to block.

Sew sleeve seams.

Sew side seams.

Work 1 row single crochet around the neckline and front opening.

Embellishments

Work chain st or other embroidery sts as desired around neck opening, as shown in the model.

Attach a few tiny buttons to the knitting.

TIP: Buttons can be tied on with embroidery floss knotted on the surface of the knitting and the ends of the floss left free; or try sewing the buttons on with different colored threads.

Work a few French knots or add beads to the embellished area as desired.

Thread a tapestry needle or bodkin with the desired length of ribbon or cord, and weave evenly around the neckline, adding beads at the ends, if desired.

Tie knots to finish off the ribbon ends and secure the beads.

Darn in any loose ends.

52

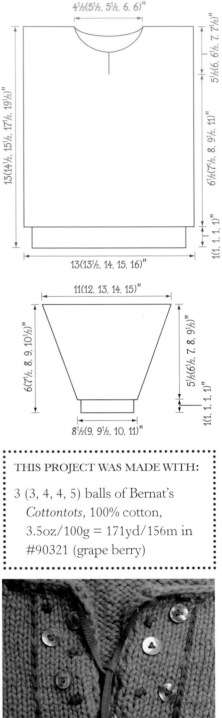

THIS PROJECT WAS MADE WITH:

3 (3, 4, 4, 5) balls of Bernat's *Cottontots*, 100% cotton, 3.5oz/100g = 171yd/156m in #90321 (grape berry)

Bugsy Scarf

Kids love a scarf like this—the pockets warm their hands and can also hold their special treasures. My Bugsy has knobby knees and bulging eyes—you can make yours just like him, or embellish him as you like!

EXPERIENCE
LEVEL
Easy

Finished Measurements

Approx 6 x 60"/15 x 152cm

Materials

Approx total: 160yd/147m chunky weight yarn*

Knitting needles: size 5.5 mm (9 U.S.) or size needed to obtain gauge

2 large buttons

2 smaller buttons

Tapestry needle

Scraps of yarn for embroidery

Approx 15"/38cm of cord for the feelers

A few yards of worsted weight yarn for the legs

Double-pointed needles (dpn) in size to work yarn for legs

4 bells

NOTE: Yarn is a matter of personal choice; two strands of worsted-weight yarn held together work well.

Gauge

14 sts = 4"/10cm in garter st

Always take time to check gauge.

shown, using a suitable scrap of yarn.

The feelers are made from 2 pieces of purchased cord. Tie knots on the ends. Sew feelers down securely on inside of pockets.

To make the legs, with yarn of your choice and double-pointed needles of the appropriate size, knit 2 cords of about 8"/20cm long for each pocket (see box, right). Attach bells firmly to the end of each cord. Tie a knot in each cord approx 2"/5cm above the bell for Bugsy's knees. Sew 2 of his funny little legs to the base of each pocket. Weave in any loose ends.

NOTE: If the scarf is for a very young child, embroider the eyes and don't use buttons, bells, or long lengths of cord.

Knitted cord, often called I-cord, is easy to make and can be used in a variety of ways. To make it, use dpn (of a size suitable for the yarn) to cast on the required number of stitches (3-5 stitches is a useful number). Knit all the stitches. Don't turn the needle. Slide the stitches to the other end of the needle and knit, pulling the yarn tightly across the back. Repeat until the cord is the desired length. Bind off all the stitches, or cut the yarn, thread a large-eyed needle and draw up the stitches tightly. Fasten off.

Instructions

CO 20 sts. Work in garter st for approx 60"/152cm. BO.

FINISHING
Fold up 4"/10cm along the scarf ends and sew securely to make pockets.

Sew on buttons for the eyes at the upper edge of pocket.

NOTE: You can have huge fun here. My Bugsy's eyes are stacked buttons, with French knots.

Thread a tapestry needle and embroider the nose and mouth as

THIS PROJECT WAS MADE WITH:

1 ball of Patons' *Shetland Chunky Tweed*, 67% acrylic/25% wool/8% rayon, 3.5oz/100g = 165yd/150m in #67532 (deep red tweed)

Miss Firecracker Sweater

he novelty yarn edgings and textured stitch pattern give this sweater the extra spark that makes it really special. Knitted in one piece to the underarm, it's also a piece of cake to make.

EXPERIENCE
LEVEL
....
Intermediate

Sizes

3 (4, 6, 8, 10) years

Finished Measurements

Chest: 26 (27, 28, 30, 32)"/66 (68.5, 71, 76, 81.5)cm

Length: 13 (14½, 15½, 17½, 19½)"/33 (36, 39.5, 44.5, 49.5)cm

Materials

Approx total: 394 (591, 591, 591, 788)yd/360 (540, 540, 540, 720)m worsted weight yarn in A and 39yd/36m novelty fur yarn in B

Knitting needles: size 5 mm (8 U.S.) *or size needed to obtain gauge*

Markers

Stitch holders

Tapestry needle

Gauge

18 sts and 24 rows = 4"/10cm in St st using A

Always take time to check gauge.

Pattern Stitch

Row 1: K

Row 2: P

Row 3: K1, p1

Row 4: P

Rep Rows 1–4

Instructions

BACK

Using B, CO 58 (60, 64, 68, 72) sts. K 5 rows (3 garter st ridges).

Cut B, join in A. Work in pat st until piece measures 7½ (10, 11, 12½, 14)"/19 (25.5, 28, 31.5, 35.5)cm from beg, ending with a WS row.

Armhole Shaping

BO 5 sts at beg of next 2 rows.

Dec 1 st each side every other row, 4 (4, 4, 4, 5) times—40 (42, 46, 50, 52) sts.

Cont in pat until piece measures 12 (13½, 14½, 16½, 18½)"/30.5 (34.5, 37, 42, 47)cm from beg, ending with a WS row.

Shoulder and Neck Shaping

Mark center 18 (22, 24, 26, 26) sts.

Next row (RS): BO 3 (3, 3, 3, 4) sts, work to end of row.

Next row (WS): BO 3 (3, 3, 3, 4) sts, work to marker, join in a second ball of yarn, work center 18 (22, 24, 26, 26) sts and slip them onto a holder, work to end of row.

Working both sides at the same time, BO at each shoulder edge every other row, 3 (3, 3, 4, 4) sts once and, AT THE SAME TIME, dec 1 st at each neck edge once.

BO 4 (3, 4, 4, 4) sts.

FRONT

Work as for back until piece measures 10 (12, 12½, 14½, 16½)"/25.5 (30.5, 31.5, 37, 42)cm from beg, ending with a WS row.

Neck Shaping

Next row (RS): Work 15 (15, 17, 19, 19) sts, join in a second ball of yarn, work center 10 (12, 12, 12, 14) sts and leave them on a holder, work to end of row.

Working both sides at the same time, BO 2 sts at each neck edge every other row, 1 (1, 2, 2, 2) times. Dec 1 st at each neck edge every other row, 3 (4, 3, 4, 3) times—10 (9, 10, 11, 12) sts. Cont in pat until piece measures 12 (13½, 14½, 16½, 18½)"/30.5 (34.5, 37, 42, 47)cm from beg.

Shoulder Shaping

Shape shoulders as for the back.

SLEEVES

With B, CO 30 (32, 34, 36, 38) sts. K 5 rows (3 garter st ridges).

Cut B. Join in A and work in pat.

Sleeve Shaping

Keeping pat correct, inc 1 st each side every 6th row, 5 (7, 8, 9, 10) times—40 (46, 50, 54, 58) sts. Cont in pat until sleeve measures 7½ (10, 11, 12 1/2, 14)"/19 (25.5, 28, 31.5, 35.5)cm from beg, ending with a WS row.

Cap Shaping

BO 5 sts at beg of next 2 rows.

Dec 1 st at each side every other row, 4 (4, 4, 4, 5) times, then every row, 3 (5, 7, 9, 9) times.

BO 1 (1, 2, 2, 2) sts at beg of next 4 rows.

BO rem 12 (14, 10, 10, 12) sts.

FINISHING

Block pieces.

Seam first shoulder.

NECKBAND

With RS facing and using A, pick up and k approx 56 (64, 68, 74, 76) sts around neck edge, including sts on holders.

Change to B and work in garter st (k all rows) for 1"/2.5cm.

BO loosely.

Seam second shoulder and neckband.

Set in sleeves.

Sew side and sleeve seams.

Darn in loose ends.

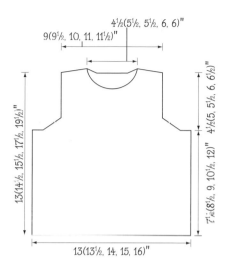

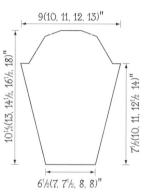

THIS PROJECT WAS MADE WITH:

2 (3, 3, 3, 4) balls of Lion Brand's *Wool-Ease Worsted Weight*, 80% acrylic/20% wool, 3oz/85g = 197yd/180m in #620-102 (ranch red) (A) and 1 ball of Lion's Brand *Fancy Fur* in #213(rainbow red) B

C risp stripes and a subtle stitch pattern
combine to give this classic sweater a
tailored edge, making it practical for both
casual and dressier wear. The colors are a
matter of personal choice—use fewer if
you prefer. The leftover yarns are more
than enough for a striped scarf, but if you
choose to knit a solid-color scarf, you'll
need only one more ball of the appropriate
color. Make one of each and you'll have a
matching father and son set.

Back-to-School Sweater and Scarf Set

Sizes

3 (4, 6, 8, 10) years

Finished Measurements

Chest: 26 (27, 28, 30, 32)"/66 (68.5, 71, 76, 81.5)cm

Length: 13 (14, 15½, 17½, 19½"/33 (35.5, 39.5, 44.5, 49.5)cm

Materials

Approx total: 200yd/183m each of A, B, C, D, E, F, and G worsted weight yarn

Knitting needles: size 4.5 mm (7 U.S.) and size 5.5 mm (9 U.S.) *or size needed to obtain gauge*

Circular knitting needle: size 4.5 mm (7 U.S.), 24"/61cm long

Stitch holders

Stitch markers

Tapestry needle

Gauge

18 sts and 24 rows = 4"/10cm in St st using larger needles

Always take time to check gauge.

Pattern Stitch

(multiple of 6 sts)

Row 1 (RS): K

Row 2: *K1, p5; rep from *

Rep Rows 1 and 2 for pat

STRIPE SEQUENCE

Rows 1–6: B.

Rows 7–8: C.

Rows 9–12: D.

Rows 13–14: E.

Rows 15–16: F.

Rows 17–20: B.

Rows 21–26: G.

Rows 27–28: A.

Rep Rows 1–28.

Instructions

BACK

Using smaller needles and A, CO 59 (61, 65, 69, 73) sts. Work in k1, p1 rib for 1½ (2, 2, 2, 2)"/4 (5, 5, 5)cm. Change to larger needles.

Work in stripe sequence and establish pat as follows:

Row 1 (RS): K.

Row 2: P5 (6, 2, 4, 6), *k1, p5; rep from * to last 6 (7, 3, 5, 7) sts, k1, p5 (6, 2, 4, 6).

Cont in stripe sequence and pat as est until piece measures 7½ (8½, 9, 10½, 12)"/19 (21.5, 23, 26.5, 30.5)cm from beg, carrying yarns not in use loosely along side of work where possible. Place markers for underarm.

Cont until piece measures 13 (14½, 15½, 17½, 19½)"/33 (37, 39.5, 44.5, 49.5)cm from beg, ending with a WS row.

Shoulder Shaping

Next row (RS): BO 19 (19, 20, 21, 22) shoulder sts and cut yarn, slip next 21 (23, 25, 27, 29) sts onto a holder for back neck, rejoin yarn and BO rem 19 (19, 20, 21, 22) shoulder sts.

FRONT

Work as for back until piece measures 7½ (8½, 9, 10½, 12)"/19 (21.5, 23, 26.5, 30.5)cm from the beg, ending with a WS row.

Neck Shaping

Next row (RS): Work 29 (30, 32, 34, 36) sts, join a new ball of yarn,

k2tog, work rem 28 (29, 31, 33, 35) sts.

Work both sides at the same time, maintaining stripe sequence and est pat, dec 1 st at neck edge every other row 7 (8, 9, 9, 9) times, then every 4 rows, 3 (3, 3, 4, 5) times.

Cont until piece measures same as back, ending so that stripe sequence matches.

BO rem 19 (19, 20, 21, 22) shoulder sts.

SLEEVES

Using A and smaller needles, CO 28 (30, 32, 34, 36) sts. Work in k1, p1 rib for 1½ (2, 2, 2, 2)"/4 (5, 5, 5, 5)cm. Change to larger needles.

Work in stripe sequence and est pat as follows:

Row 1 (RS): K1, M1, k13 (14, 15, 16, 17) sts, M1, k13 (14, 15, 16, 17) sts, M1, k1—31 (33, 35, 37, 39) sts.

Row 2: P3 (4, 5, 6, 1), *k1, p5; rep from * to the last 4 (5, 6, 7, 2) sts, k1, p3 (4, 5, 6, 1) sts.

Sleeve shaping

Note: Work incs 1 st in from edge as follows:

Size 3 only: Inc 1 st on each side every 3 rows, 10 times.

Sizes (4, 6, 8, 10) only: Inc 1 st on each side every 2 rows (1, 0, 0, 0) times, then every 4 rows (10, 12, 14, 15) times, making sure you keep pat correct as new sts are added.

All sizes: There will be 51 (55, 59, 65, 69) sts on needle.

Cont in pat until the sleeve measures 7½ (10, 11, 12½, 14)"/19 (25.5, 28, 31.5, 35.5)cm from beg.

BO loosely.

FINISHING
Block pieces.

Sew shoulder seams.

NECKBAND
With RS facing, using circular needle and A, pick up and k30 (33, 35, 37, 39) sts along right front, 21 (23, 25, 27, 29) sts from back holder, and 30 (33, 35, 37, 39) sts along left front neck—81 (89, 95, 101, 107) sts. Do not join.

Work back and forth in k1, p1 rib for 1"/2.5cm.

BO loosely in rib.

Overlap neckband edges at center front and stitch neatly in place.

Pin sleeves in position between markers and sew in place

Pin sleeve and side seams together, matching stripes carefully.

Sew seams using mattress stitch.

Darn in all loose yarn ends neatly.

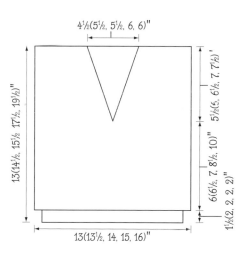

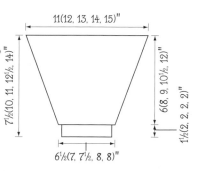

SOLID-COLOR SCARF

Finished Measurements

Approx 6 x 42"/15 x 106.5cm

Materials

Approx total: 200yd/183m in color of choice worsted weight yarn

Knitting needles: size 5.5 mm (9 U.S.) *or size needed to obtain gauge*

Gauge

24 sts = 4"/10 cm in pat st (gauge is not critical)

Pattern Stitch

MISTAKE STITCH RIB
(multiple of 4 sts + 1)

Every row: *K2, p2; rep from* to last st, k1

Instructions

Using larger needles, CO 37 sts. Work in pat st for approx 42"/106.5cm, or until there is just enough yarn left to BO sts.

BO in pat st.

FINISHING
Weave in loose ends.

EXPERIENCE
LEVEL
Easy

STRIPED SCARF

THESE PROJECTS WERE
MADE WITH:

1 ball each of Plymouth Yarn's *Encore Worsted Weight*, 75% acrylic/25% wool, 3.5oz/100g = 200yd/183m in #240 (A), #1604 (B), #1014 (C), #174 (D), #133 (E), #1383 (F), and #1204 (G)

1 ball extra of color of choice for solid-color scarf

Finished Measurements

Approx 9 x 72"/23 x 183cm (with ends unknotted)

Materials

Oddments of the colors used in the sweater

Knitting needles: size 5.5 mm (9 U.S.) *or size needed to obtain gauge*

Gauge

18 sts and 24 rows = 4"/10cm in St st

Always take time to check gauge.

NOTE: The scarf is designed so that the edges roll inward.

Instructions

Using larger needles and color of choice, CO 40 sts.

Work random stripes in St st for 72"/183cm or desired length.

BO loosely.

FINISHING

Block lightly.

Weave in loose ends.

Tie a jaunty knot at each end of the scarf.

EXPERIENCE
LEVEL
Easy

Ribbons and ruffles adorn this stylish jacket, rosebuds trim the dainty bag. It won't take you long to turn that special little girl into a fairytale princess as this outfit is designed for quick knitting. The jacket is worked in one piece to the armhole, the ruffle is worked separately and knitted on, and the bag is knitted in the round, so there's very little finishing.

EXPERIENCE
LEVEL
....
Intermediate

Pretty Princess Jacket and Purse Set

JACKET

BODY

Using the smaller needle, cast on 77(80, 86, 89, 95) sts and k5 rows.

(RS): Change to the larger needle and work in St st until the piece measures 3 (4, 4, 5, 5)"/7.5(10.2, 10.2, 12.7, 12.7)cm.

Eyelet row
(RS): k2, *yo, k2 tog, k1; repeat from * to the end.

Continue in St st until the piece measures 7½ (8½, 9, 10½, 12)"/19(21.6, 22.9, 26.7, 30.5)cm from the beg.

Divide for fronts and back

RIGHT FRONT

(RS): K19 (20, 21, 22, 24) sts and place the rest of the sts on a holder.

(WS): BO 2 (2, 3, 3, 3) sts and purl to the end of the row.

Begin neck shaping
Dec 1 st at neck edge every 2 rows 1 (2, 1, 1, 1) times, then every 4

rows 6 (6, 7, 8, 9) times—10 (10, 10, 10, 11) sts.

Continue working until the piece measures 13(14½, 15½, 17½, 19½)"/33(37, 39.5, 44.5, 49.5)cm from the beg.

Leave the sts on a holder.

BACK

Place the next 39 (40, 44, 45, 47) sts back onto the needle, join in the yarn and BO 2 (2, 3, 3, 3)sts at the beg of the next two rows—35 (36, 38, 39, 41) sts.

Work until the piece measures 13(14½, 15½, 17½, 19½)"/33(37, 39.5, 44.5, 49.5)cm from the beg.

Place 10 (10, 10, 10, 11) sts at each side on separate holders for the shoulders.

Place the 15 (16, 18, 19, 19) back neck sts on a holder.

LEFT FRONT

Place the rem 19 (20, 21, 22, 24) sts onto the needle, join in the yarn,

66

and complete to match the right front, reversing all shapings.

SLEEVES

Using the larger needle, cast on 40 (46, 46, 52, 52) sts for the ruffle and work one inch in St st.

Next row (RS): *k2tog to end—20 (23, 23, 26, 26) sts.

Work 3 more rows in St st.

Eyelet row

(RS): k2, *yo, k2tog, k1 to end.

P 1 row.

Inc 1 st on each side every 4 rows 5 (0, 2, 0, 0) times, then every 6 rows 2 (7, 7, 9, 10) times—34(37, 41, 44, 46) sts.

Continue working until sleeve measures 7½ (10, 11, 12, 13)"/19(25.4, 27.9, 30.5, 33)cm from the eyelet row.

BO loosely.

FINISHING

Slip each set of shoulder sts on separate needles and work a 3-needle BO.

Front Bands

Using smaller needle, beg at right lower edge, pick up and knit 34 (40, 42, 48, 54) sts to the start of the neck shaping, 24 (26, 27, 30, 33) along the right neck edge, knit the 15 (16, 18, 19, 19)sts from the holder, pick up and knit 24 (26, 27, 30, 33) along the left neck edge, and 34 (40, 42, 48, 54) sts to the lower edge—131 (148, 156, 175, 193) sts

Knit 3 rows.

RUFFLE

NOTES: The ruffle extends along the right front band from the eyelet row at the waist, across the back neck, and along the left front band to the eyelet row. It is knitted separately and then joined to the front band, using a 3rd needle.

Place markers at the front edges at the row of eyelets.

Count the number of sts on the needle between the markers.

Using a separate ball of yarn and the larger needle, cast on DOUBLE this number of sts for the ruffle.

Work in St st until the ruffle measures 2"/5cm.

(RS): *k2tog to end.

NOTE: Check that the number of sts left on the needle is the same as the number on the front bands between the markers. Adjust if needed. Purl one row.

Attach ruffle

Next row (RS): K to the marker on the right front band. Place the ruffle with RS facing so that the two needles are parallel to each other. Insert the needle into the first ruffle stitch and knit it together with the next stitch on the needle for the front band. Repeat this all around the front band until the ruffle is attached between the row of eyelets. Continue knitting the rem front band sts to the end of the row.

BO all the sts loosely..

Sew the sleeve seams.

Pin sleeves into armholes and sew.

Darn in any loose ends.

Cut 2 lengths of ribbon each about 20 ins long and thread with the bodkin through the sleeve ruffles. Draw up to fit and tie bows.

Thread ribbon through the eyelets at waist.

BAG

NOTE: Change to the 16"/41cm needle and then the dpns when it becomes necessary.

Using the 24"/61cm circular needle, cast on 80 sts and join, being careful not to twist.

Place marker. K every round until the work measures 2"/5cm.

Dec round: *k2tog to the end of the round—40sts

Knit one more round.

Eyelet round

k1, *yo, k2tog, k1 to the end of the round.

Continue working in rounds until the piece measures 8"/20.3 cm

Bag shaping

1st dec row: *k 6, k2tog to the end of the rnd—35 sts

Next and every other round: k.

2nd dec row: *k 5, k2tog to the end of the rnd—30 sts.

3rd dec row: *k4, k2tog to the end of the rnd—25 sts.

Continue decreasing 5 sts in each dec round until 10 sts rem.

Next round: *k2 tog to end of rnd —5 sts. Cut yarn, thread a tapestry needle and draw through the sts. Fasten off securely.

FINISHING

Darn in loose ends.

Sew rosebuds on the bag as desired.

With the yarn held double, crochet two cords in chain stitch of approx 30"/76 cm each, or use ribbon if you prefer.

Thread one cord from right to left through the eyelets, and the other from left to right.

Knot the ends. Pull up cords to close the bag.

THESE PROJECTS WERE MADE WITH:

Knit One, Crochet Too *Fleece* (approx 109yds/100m) 4 (4, 5, 6, 7) balls # 602 Sky

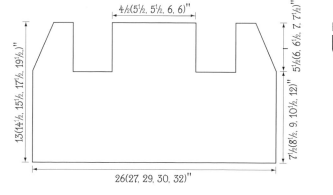

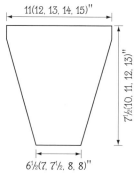

his quick-to-knit sweaterdress is a versatile addition to a young lady's wardrobe. It looks great with brightly colored tights, but it can also be worn over a skirt or pants. The lace-up front detail adds style and comfort and makes the piece easy to pull on and off.

Boucle Sweaterdress

Sizes

3 (4, 6, 8, 10) years

Finished Measurements

Chest: 26 (27, 28, 30, 32)"/66 (68.5, 71, 76, 81.5)cm

Length: 19 (20, 21, 23, 25)"/48.5 (51, 53.5, 58.5, 63.5)cm

Materials

Approx total: 275 (330, 385, 440, 495)yd/252 (302, 352, 402, 452)m bulky weight yarn

Knitting needles: size 6 mm (10 U.S.) and size 8 mm (11 U.S.) *or size needed to obtain gauge*

Stitch holders

Ribbon or cord

Tapestry needle or bodkin

Beads (optional)

Gauge

10 sts and 16 rows = 4"/10cm in reverse St st using larger needles

Always take time to check gauge.

Pattern Stitch

REV ST ST

Row 1: (RS) P

Row 2: K

Rep rows 1 and 2

Instructions

BACK

Using smaller needles, CO 34 (36, 38, 40, 42) sts. K 8 rows (4 garter st ridges).

Change to larger needles and reverse St st. Work until piece measures 6 (6, 7, 7, 8)"/15 (15, 18, 18, 20.5)cm from beg, ending with a WS row.

Next row (RS): Dec 1 st at each side—32 (34, 36, 38, 40) sts.

Cont until piece measures 14½ (15, 15½, 17, 18½)"/37 (38, 39.5, 43, 47)cm from beg, ending with a WS row.

Armhole Shaping

BO 3 sts at beg of next 2 rows.

Dec 1 st at each side every other row, 2 times—22 (24, 26, 28, 30) sts.

Cont until piece measures 17½ (18½, 19½, 21½, 23½)"/44.5 (47, 49.5, 54.5, 59.5) cm from beg, ending with a WS row.

Neck Shaping

Next row (RS): Work 6 (6, 7, 7, 8) sts, join another ball of yarn, work 10 (12, 12, 14, 14) sts and place on a holder for back neck, work 6 (6, 7, 7, 8) sts.

Working both sides at the same time, work 1 more row.

Next row: Dec 1 st at each neck edge.

BO rem 5 (5, 6, 6, 7) sts on each shoulder.

FRONT

Work as for back until beg of armhole shaping, ending with a WS row—32 (34, 36, 38, 40) sts.

Armhole and Neck Shaping

Next row (RS): BO 3 sts, p10 (11, 12, 13, 14) sts, k3, and place rem sts on a holder.

Turn work.

LEFT FRONT

Cont to shape armhole as for back, then cont working until piece measures 16 (17, 18, 20, 22)"/40.5 (43, 45.5, 51, 56)cm from CO edge; AT THE SAME TIME, keep 3 sts in garter st at neck opening to form front band, ending with a RS row.

Neck Shaping

Next row (WS): At neck edge, place 5 (6, 6, 6, 6) sts on a holder for neckband and work to end of row.

Dec 1 st at neck edge every other row 1 (1, 1, 2, 2) times.

Cont until piece measures same as back to shoulder.

BO rem 5 (5, 6, 6, 7) shoulder sts.

RIGHT FRONT

Return to sts on holder and place them on needle.

RS: Join yarn and k first 3 sts, p to end of row.

Next row (WS): BO first 3 sts for armhole shaping, finish row.

Complete right front to match left front, reversing all shaping.

SLEEVES

Using smaller needles, CO 16 (18, 20, 20, 22) sts. K 8 rows (4 garter st ridges).

Change to larger needles and reverse St st.

Sleeve Shaping

Inc 1 st each side every 6 (7, 8, 7, 8) rows, 3 (4, 4, 5, 5) times—22 (26, 28, 30, 32) sts.

Cont in reverse St st until sleeve measures 7½ (10, 11, 12½, 13½)"/19 (25.5, 28, 31.5, 34.5)cm from beg, ending with a WS row.

Cap Shaping

BO 3 sts at beg of next 2 rows.

Dec 1 st at each side every other row, 2 times.

Dec 1 st at each side every row, 1 (2, 4, 5, 6) times.

BO 0 (1, 1, 1, 1) st at beg of next 0 (4, 4, 4, 4) rows.

BO rem 10 (8, 6, 6, 6) sts.

FINISHING

Block pieces lightly by spraying with water.

Join shoulder seams.

Neckband

With smaller needles, beg at right front edge, k5 (6, 6, 6, 6) sts from holder, pick up and k11 (11, 12, 12, 12) sts from side neck, k10 (12, 12, 14, 14) sts from back neck holder, pick up and k11 (11, 12, 12, 12) from side neck, and k5 (6, 6, 6, 6) from holder—42 (46, 48, 50, 50) sts.

Work in garter st for 1"/2.5cm.

BO loosely.

Sew sleeves and side seams.

Pin sleeves into position at armholes and sew neatly in place.

Cut the desired length of ribbon or cord and thread through a tapestry needle or bodkin.

Starting at bottom of neck opening, lace across both sides of front opening as you would a shoe.

Thread beads on ends of ribbon or cord (optional) and tie knots to finish off the ends.

Darn in any loose ends.

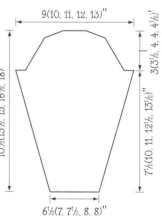

THIS PROJECT WAS MADE WITH:

5 (6, 7, 8, 9) balls of Lion Brand's *Watercolors*, 65% acrylic/35% wool, 1.75oz/50g = 55yd/50m in #980-352 (mist gray)

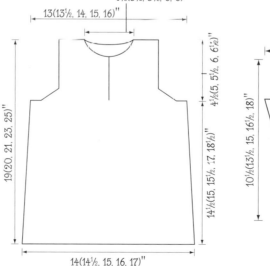

S houlder flanges and stripes combine in this sweater to create a winning formula. Kids love the comfort and simplicity; moms love how easy it is to make.

EXPERIENCE
LEVEL
....
Intermediate

Racing Stripes Sweater

Sizes

3 (4, 6, 8, 10) years

Finished Measurements

Chest: 26 (27, 29, 30, 32)"/66 (68.5, 73.5, 76, 81.5)cm

Length: 14 (15½, 16½, 18½, 20½)"/35.5 (39.5, 42, 47, 52)cm

Materials

Approx total: 286 (429, 429, 572, 715)yd/161 (392, 392, 522, 467)m in A and 143yd/130m in B chunky weight yarn

Knitting needles: size 5 mm (8 U.S.) and size 6 mm (10 U.S.) *or size needed to obtain gauge*

Circular knitting needle: size 5 mm (8 U.S.), 16"/40cm long

Stitch holders

Stitch markers

Tapestry needle

Gauge

14 sts and 20 rows = 4"/10cm in St st using larger needles

Always take time to check gauge.

Stripe Sequence

(10 rows)

Rows 1–2: B

Rows 3–4: A

Instructions

BACK

Using A and smaller needles, CO 46 (46, 50, 50, 54) sts. Work in k2, p2 rib for 1½ (2, 2, 2, 2)"/4 (5, 5, 5, 5)cm.

Change to larger needles. Working in St st, inc 1 st at beg and end of first row for sizes 4, 8, and 10 only—46 (48, 50, 52, 56) sts.

Work straight in St st until piece measures 7½ (8½, 9, 10½, 12)"/19 (21.5, 23, 26.5, 30.5)cm from beg, ending with a WS row.

Join in B and work stripe sequence for 10 rows. Cut B.

Place markers for underarm.

Cont working in A only until piece measures 13½ (15, 16, 18, 20)"/34.5 (38, 40.5, 45.5, 51)cm from beg, ending with a WS row.

Neck Shaping

Next row (RS): Work 15 (15, 16, 16, 18) sts, join another ball of yarn, work 16 (18, 18, 20, 20) sts and place them on a holder for back neck, work to end of row.

Working both sides at the same time, dec 1 st at each neck edge.

Cont until piece measures 14 (15½, 16½, 18½, 20½)"/35.5 (39.5, 42, 47, 52)cm from beg.

Leave rem 14 (14, 15, 15, 17) sts on separate holders for shoulders.

FRONT

Work as for back until piece measures 11½ (13, 14, 15½, 17½)"/29 (33, 35.5, 39.5, 44.5)cm from beg, ending with a WS row.

Neck Shaping

Next row (RS): Work 18 (18, 20, 20, 23) sts, join another ball of yarn, work 10 (12, 10, 12, 10) sts and place them on a holder for front neck, work to end of row.

Working both sides at the same time, BO 2 sts at each neck edge.

Dec 1 st at each neck edge every other row, 2 (2, 3, 3, 4) times.

Cont until front measures same as back to shoulders.

Leave rem 14 (14, 15, 15, 17) sts on separate holders for shoulders.

SLEEVES

Using A and smaller needles, CO 22 (22, 26, 26, 30) sts. Work in k2, p2 rib for 1½ (2, 2, 2, 2)"/4 (5, 5, 5, 5)cm.

Change to larger needles. Work in St st, inc 1 st at beg and end of first row for sizes 3, 4, and 8 only—24 (24, 26, 28, 30) sts.

Sleeve Shaping

Size 3 only: Inc 1 st each side every 2nd row once, then every 4th row 6 times.

Size 4 only: Inc 1 st each side every 4th row, 9 times.

Sizes 6, 8, and 10: Inc 1 st each side every 4 rows, 9 (9, 5) times, then every 6 rows, 1 (2, 6) times.

All sizes: There will be 38 (42, 46, 50, 52) sts on needle.

Work straight until sleeve measures 7½ (10, 11, 12½, 14)"/19 (25.5, 28, 31.5, 35.5)cm from beg.

BO sts.

FINISHING

Block pieces to measurements.

Place shoulder sts on separate needles and join using 3-needle BO.

NECKBAND

With RS facing, using circular needle and A, pick up and k approx 48 (56, 58, 64, 68) sts around neck, including sts on holders. Adjust number of sts, if necessary, so that total is a multiple of 4 to ensure that k2, p2 rib pat remains correct.

Work around in k2, p2 rib for 1"/2.5cm.

BO loosely in rib.

FLANGES

With RS facing, using smaller needles and B, pick up and k44 (48, 52, 56, 60) sts between under-arm markers.

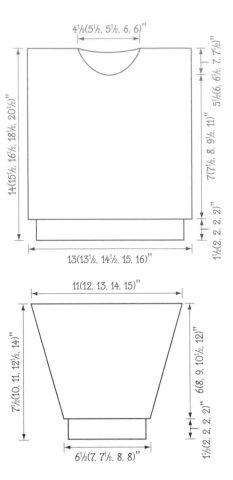

Work in k2, p2 rib for 1"/2.5cm.

BO loosely in rib.

Pin top of sleeves in place under the flanges and sew seams.

Sew sleeve and side seams.

Sew flange seams.

Darn in loose ends.

THIS PROJECT WAS MADE WITH:

2 (3, 3, 4, 5) balls of Plymouth Yarn's *Encore Chunky*, 75% acrylic/25% wool, 3.5oz/100g = 143yd/130m in #389 (A) and 1 ball in #1382 (B)

74

Lemonade Top

EXPERIENCE
LEVEL
·········
Intermediate

A s cool and refreshing as the drink it's named

for, this short-sleeve top is just the thing for

late spring at school or summer in the park. The

shape is simple, but the texture makes it really shine.

Sizes

3 (4, 6, 8, 10) years

Finished Measurements

Chest: 26 (27, 28, 29, 30)"/66
(68.5, 71, 73.5, 76)cm

Length: 12 (13, 14, 16, 18)"/30.5
(33, 35.5, 40.5, 45.5)cm

Materials

Approx total: 405 (510, 590, 695,
830)yd/370 (466, 539, 635,
759)m worsted weight yarn,
100% cotton

Knitting needles: size 4 mm (6
U.S.) and size 4.5 mm (7 U.S.)
or size needed to obtain gauge

Stitch markers

Stitch holders

Tapestry needle

Gauge

20 sts and 28 rows = 4"/10cm in
pat st using larger needles

20 sts and 26 rows = 4"/10cm in
St st using larger needles

Always take time to check gauge.

Pattern Stitch

Row 1 (RS): K

Row 2: P

Rows 3–4: K1, *(k1, yo, k2tog),
repeat from * to last st, k

Rep Rows 1–4

Instructions

BACK

With smaller needles, CO 65 (68,
71, 74, 77) sts. K 5 rows, counting
CO row as Row 1 (3 garter st
ridges).

Change to larger needles. Beg on
RS, work in pat st until piece
measures 6 (7, 7, 9, 10 1/2)"/15
(18, 18, 23, 25.5)cm from beg.

Place markers for underarm seams.

Cont in pat until piece measures 10½
(11, 12, 14, 15½)"/26.5 (28, 30.5,
35.5, 39.5)cm from beg, ending
with a 4th pat row.

Neck Shaping

Next row (RS): Work 18 (18, 19, 19,
20) sts, attach another ball of yarn
and work next 29 (32, 33, 36, 37)
sts, slipping them onto a holder,
then work to end of row.

Working both sides at the same
time, dec 1 st at each neck edge on
next row.

Keeping pat correct, cont until piece
measures 12 (13, 14, 16, 18)"/30.5
(33, 35.5, 40.5, 45.5)cm from beg,
ending with a p row.

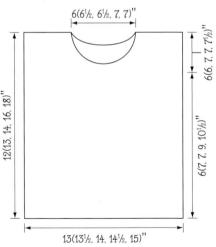

6(6½, 6½, 7, 7)"

6(6, 7, 7, 7½)"

6(7, 7, 9, 10½)"

12(13, 14, 16, 18)"

13(13½, 14, 14½, 15)"

BO 17 (17, 18, 18, 19) sts on each
shoulder.

FRONT

Work as for back until piece measures 8½ (9, 10, 12, 13½)"/21.5 (23,
25.5, 30.5, 34.5)cm from beg, ending with a 4th pat row.

Neck Shaping

Next row (RS): Work
21 (21, 22, 22, 23)
sts, attach anoth
er ball of yarn,
work next 23
(26, 27, 30, 31)
sts and slip
them onto a
holder, then
work to end of
row.

BO 2 sts at each neck edge
once.

Keeping pat correct, dec 1 st at each
neck edge every other row, 2
times.

Cont in pat until piece measures
same as back to shoulder.

BO 17 (17, 18, 18, 19) rem shoulder
sts.

FINISHING
Seam first shoulder.

NECKBAND
With RS facing and using smaller
needles, pick up and k approx 78
(84, 90, 96, 100) sts evenly around
neck edge, including sts from
holders.

K 4 rows.

BO all sts.

Sew neckband and second shoulder
seam.

ARMBANDS
With RS facing and using smaller
needles, pick up and k approx
46 (46, 56, 56, 62) sts
between underarm
markers.

K 4 rows.

BO all sts.

Sew side and underarm
seams.

Weave in any loose
ends.

THIS PROJECT WAS MADE WITH:

3 (3, 3, 4, 5) balls of Bernat's
  Cottontots, 100% cotton,
  3.5oz/100g = 171yd/156m in
  #90616 (lemon berry)

The dots of jewel-tone color in this smart cardigan add a cheerful note to even the dreariest winter day. It's knitted in one piece to the armhole, and the front bands are worked in garter stitch as the work progresses, so very little finishing is required. This project features a kilt pin closure, but you may have some other ideas.

ColorSplash Cardigan

Sizes

3 (4, 6, 8, 10) years

Finished Measurements

Chest: 28 (29, 31, 32, 34)"/71 (73.5, 79, 81.5, 86.5)cm

Length: 15 (17, 19, 20½, 21)"/38 (43, 48.5, 52, 53.5)cm

Materials

Approx total: 284 (355, 426, 497, 568)yd/260 (324, 389, 454, 519)m of a bulky, textured yarn

Knitting needles: size 6.5 mm (10½ U.S.) *or size needed to obtain gauge*

Stitch holders

Tapestry needle

Decorative pin for the closure

NOTE: A circular knitting needle size 6.5 mm (10½ U.S.), 24"/61cm long, will accommodate the body stitches more easily, but is not essential.

Gauge

12 sts and 19 rows = 4"/10cm in reverse St st

Always take time to check gauge.

Pattern Stitch

REV ST ST

Row 1: (RS) P

Row 2: K

Rep rows 1 and 2

Instructions

BODY

CO 86 (90, 94, 98, 106) sts. K 8 rows (4 garter st ridges).

Next row (RS): K5, p to last 5 sts, k5.

Cont in rev St st, working first 5 and last 5 sts in garter st (k every row) for front bands, until piece measures 10 (11½, 13, 14, 14)"/25.5 (29, 33, 35.5, 35.5)cm from beg, ending with a WS row.

Divide for fronts and back

Next row (RS): K5 sts of front band, p19 (20, 21, 22, 24) sts, and place rem sts on a spare needle or holder. Turn work.

RIGHT FRONT
Armhole and Neck Shaping

Next row (WS): BO 3 (3, 3, 3, 4) sts, k to last 7 sts, k2tog, k5—20 (21, 22, 23, 24) sts.

NOTE: Remember to keep 5 sts in garter st for front band.

Dec 1 st at armhole edge every other row, 3 times; AT THE SAME TIME, dec 1 st at neck edge every row, 6 (5, 0, 0, 0) times, then every 2nd row, 0 (2, 7, 8, 8) times —11 (11, 12, 12, 13) sts.

Cont until piece measures 15 (17, 19, 20½, 21)"/38 (43, 48.5, 52, 53.5)cm from beg.

BO 6 (6, 7, 7, 8) shoulder sts. Cont working rem 5 sts in garter st for front band for approx 2 (2½, 2½, 3, 3)"/5 (6.5, 6.5, 7.5, 7.5)cm.

Leave these 5 sts on a safety pin.

BACK

Return to sts on holder and place 38 (40, 42, 44, 48) sts on needle for back.

BO 3 (3, 3, 3, 4) sts at beg of next 2 rows.

Dec 1 st at each armhole edge every other row, 3 times—26 (28, 30, 32, 34) sts.

Cont working until back measures 15 (17, 19, 20½, 21)"/38 (43, 48.5, 52, 53.5)cm from CO edge.

BO all sts.

LEFT FRONT

Place rem 24 (25, 26, 27, 29) sts on needle.

Next row (RS): BO 3 (3, 3, 3, 4) sts, p to last 7 sts, k2tog, k5—20 (21, 22, 23, 24) sts.

Complete to match right front, reversing all shaping.

SLEEVES

CO 20 (22, 22, 24, 26) sts. K 12 rows (6 garter st ridges).

Working in rev St st, inc 1 st at each edge every 8 (8, 6, 6, 6) rows, 3 (3, 4, 1, 1) times, then every 0 (10, 8, 8, 8) rows,

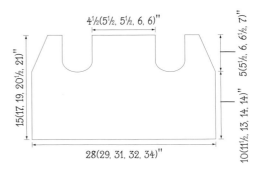

0 (1, 2, 5, 6) times—26 (30, 34, 36, 40) sts.

Cont until sleeve measures 7½ (10, 11, 12, 13)"/19 (25.5, 28, 30.5, 33)cm from beg, ending with a WS row.

Cap Shaping

BO 3 (3, 3, 3, 4) sts at beg of next 2 rows.

Dec 1 st at each side every other row, 3 times.

Dec 1 st each side every row, 1 (3, 4, 6, 8) times.

BO 1 st at beg of next 4 rows.

BO rem 8 (8, 10, 8, 6) sts.

FINISHING

Block pieces lightly by spraying with water.

Seam back and fronts together at shoulders.

Adjust length of garter st bands so that they meet at center back.

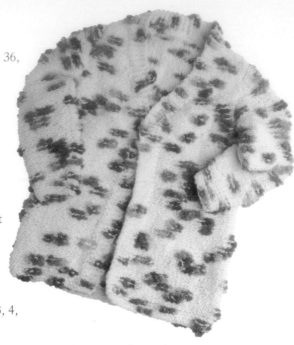

Join them together using a 3-needle BO.

Sew back neckband neatly into place.

Pin sleeves into armholes and seam in place.

Sew sleeve seams.

Darn in any loose ends.

THIS PROJECT WAS MADE WITH:

5 (6, 7, 8, 9) balls of Lion Brand's *Mystery*, 76% acrylic/24% wool, 1.75oz/50g = approx 71yd/65m in #200 (fire opal)

17(17, 18, 18, 19)"

10½(13½, 14½, 16, 17)"

7½(10, 11, 12, 13)"

6½(7, 7½, 8, 8)"

4½(5½, 5½, 6, 6)"

5(5½, 6, 6½, 7)"

15(17, 19, 20½, 21)"

10(11½, 13, 14, 14)"

28(29, 31, 32, 34)"

Treasure Pocket Vests

These snappy vests require very little finishing and are so comfy and cheerful, you'll want to make several. Kids love the bright pockets, which are designed to hold their special little treasures, such as the Pocket Pals on page 85.

as the Pocket Pals on page 85.

EXPERIENCE
LEVEL
Intermediate

Sizes

3 (4, 6, 8) years

Finished Measurements

Chest: 27 (29, 30, 32)"/68.5 (73.5, 76, 81.5)cm

Length: 14 (15½, 17½, 19½)" /35.5 (39.5, 44.5, 49.5)cm

Materials

Approx total for either version: 110 (110, 110, 220)yd/100 (100, 100, 201)m of a chunky weight yarn in A

110yd/100m each B, C, D

Knitting needles: 5 and 5.5mm (size 8 and 9 US), *or size needed to obtain gauge*

Stitch holders

Tapestry needle

Buttons (optional)

Gauge

16 sts and 22 rows = 4"/10cm in St st with larger needles

Always take time to check gauge.

VERSION 1

Instructions

BACK

Using smaller needles and A, CO 54 (58, 60, 64) sts. Work in k1, p1 rib for 1½ (2, 2, 2)" /4 (5, 5, 5)cm.

Change to larger needles. Beg on RS, work 10 rows in St st.

Join in B and work stripes as follows:

NOTE: Carry A loosely along side of work until needed; cut and join in other colors as required:

8 rows B

4 rows A

4 rows C

4 rows A

2 rows D.

Continue working in A until the piece measures 8 (9, 10½, 12)"/20.5 (23, 26.5, 30.5)cm from beg, ending with a WS row.

SLEEVE BANDS

CO 5 sts at beg of next 2 rows—64 (68, 70, 74) sts.

Continue working in St st, knitting the first and last 5 sts of each row, until the piece measures 13 (14, 16, 18)"/33 (35.5, 40.5, 45.5)cm from CO edge, ending with a RS row.

Next row (WS): K5, p13 (15, 15, 17), k28 (28, 30, 30), p13 (15, 15, 17), k5.

Next row (RS): K.

Repeat these 2 rows once, and then first of these 2 rows again.

Back Neck and Shoulder Shaping

(RS): K21 (23, 23, 25) sts, join in a second ball of yarn, BO next 22 (22, 24, 24) sts, K21 (23, 23, 25) sts.

(WS): K5, p13 (15, 15, 17), k3 on 1st set of sts; then k3, p13 (15, 15, 17), k5 on 2nd set of sts.

Continue working on both sets of shoulder sts at the same time, keeping 5 sts in garter st at sleeve edge and 3 sts in garter st at neck edge until piece measures 14½ (15½, 17½, 19½)"/37 (39.5, 44.5, 49.5)cm from beg. Place shoulder sts on separate holders.

FRONT

Work as given for the back until the piece measures 11½ (12½, 14,16)"/29 (31.5, 35.5, 40.5)cm from beg.

Front neck and shoulder shaping

Work as given for back until front measures same as back.

Place shoulder sts on separate holders.

TIP: Count the garter stitch ridges of the sleeve bands to ensure that back and front are the same length.

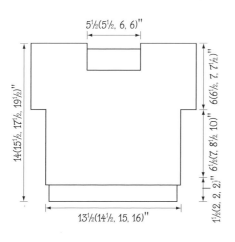

5½(5½, 6, 6)"

14(15½, 17½, 19½)"

6(6½, 7, 7½)"

6½(7, 8½, 10)"

1½(2, 2, 2)"

13½(14½, 15, 16)"

VERSION 2

Instructions

BACK

Using smaller needles and A, CO 54 (58, 60, 64) sts. Work in k1, p1 rib for 1½ (2, 2, 2)"/4 (5, 5, 5)cm.

Note: When changing colors, twist yarns at back of work to avoid creating holes

(RS): Change to larger needles and work 10 rows in St st.

Cut A, join in B and work stripes as follows:

10 rows B

8 rows D

6 rows C

2 rows B

2 rows C

2 rows B.

Join in A and complete back as given for Version 1.

FRONT

Using smaller needles and A, cast on 54 (58, 60, 64) sts. Work in k1, p1 rib for 1½ (2, 2, 2)"/4 (5, 5, 5)cm.

(RS): Cut A. Change to larger needles.

Join in C and k13 (15,15, 17) sts, join in B and k to end of row.

Next row: With B, p to last 13 (15, 15,17,17) sts, change to C and p to end of row.

(RS): Join in D, k13 (15, 15, 17) sts, change to B and k to end of row.

Continue working 3-color pat as established until piece measures approx 5"/12.5cm from beg. Keeping the 2-row stripe pat, cut B and join in A to replace the B section. Work until front measures same as back to start of sleeve bands.

(RS): Join in a second ball of A, CO 5 sts, drop A, and work stripe pat, then solid A section to end of row.

With A, CO 5 sts at beg of next row and continue stripe sequence and solid A section as before.

Complete as given for front of version 1, remembering to k the first and last 5 sts of each row for armbands, and keeping the color pat correct.

POCKETS

NOTE: The basic pocket is worked over 27 sts and has a garter st 'frame' in a contrast color. The 'frame' has 3 sts at each side edge and 3 garter st ridges at top and bottom. The St st portion of the pocket is worked over 24 rows.

Version 1

Using D and larger needles, CO 27 sts. K 5 rows.

Next row (RS): K3 with D, join in B and k21, join in a second ball of D, k3.

Maintaining garter st border in D, work 3 more rows in St st, using B.

Next row (RS): With D, k3; k6 in B; join in C and k9; k6 in B; k3 in D.

Keeping this color sequence correct, work 13 more rows in St st.

Cut C. Work 6 rows in St st with B, maintaining garter st borders in D.

Cut B.

(RS): With D, k 5 rows.

BO all sts loosely.

Version 2

Work as for Version 1 with garter stitch frame worked in D.

The St st stripes are worked as follows:

4 rows C

4 rows A

4 rows C

4 rows B.

FINISHING

Block the pieces.

Place each set of shoulder sts on separate needles and work 3-needle BO.

Sew underarm and side seams, taking care to match the stripes.

Position pocket as desired and pin in place.

Sew pocket to vest along inner side of garter sts border, using backstitch.

THIS PROJECT WAS MADE WITH:

Version 1:

1 (2, 2, 2) ball(s) of Muench's *Tessin* 43% superwash wool/35% acrylic/22% cotton 4oz/100g = 110yds/100m) in #806 (A)

All sizes: 1 ball each B #808, C #807, D #805

Version 2:

1 (2, 2, 2) ball(s) A # 827

1 (2, 2, 2) balls of Muench's *Tessin* 43% superwash wool/35% acrylic/22% cotton 4oz/100g = 110yds/100m) in #827 (A)

All sizes: 1 ball each B #885, C #824, D #857

POCKET PALS

These pocket pals are great fun to make and can tuck into a pocket or purse, hang from a backpack, serve as key rings and light pulls, or decorate a special gift. Make them with a squeaker inside to really command attention!

Finished Measurements

Approx 3 x 3"/7.5 x 7.5cm

NOTE: Finished size is a matter of choice

Materials

Yarn oddments

Knitting needles: size appropriate to yarn used

Tapestry needle

Squeakers* (optional)

Assorted findings: key ring, swivel clip, hanging loop, or large safety pin

Embellishments of your choice

Ribbon or cord (optional)

Stuffing (optional)

2 double-pointed needles (dpns): size appropriate to yarn used

*SOURCES: Hobby and craft stores or large pet chain stores, where they are sold to replace the squeakers in toys

Gauge

Gauge is not critical and will vary according to the yarn used

Instructions

BODY

With yarn and needles of choice, CO enough sts to knit a piece approx 3"/7.5cm wide.

Work in garter st (k every row) for about 6"/15cm.

BO sts.

FINISHING

Sew CO and BO edges together.

Embellish the pocket pals any way you choose.

Sew one side seam, insert the squeaker (if desired), and sew rem seam closed.

Attach a key ring, swivel clip, hanging loop, etc., or sew a large safety pin on the back.

TAIL

NOTE: These can be made from ribbon or cord, or knitted as follows:

Using yarn and color of choice and dpns in appropriate size, CO 3 sts.

Work I-cord (see box on right) for desired length.

Cut yarn and join in a new color.

Inc 1 st in each st—6 sts.

Work back and forth in St st for about 1"/2.5 cm.

Cut yarn, thread a tapestry needle, and draw tightly through all sts.

Fasten off.

Sew up the seam.

Stuff tail end lightly, if desired.

EARS

Using yarn and needles of choice, CO 10 sts. Work in garter st for 12 rows.

Next row: K2tog across row—5 sts.

Cut yarn, draw tightly through rem 5 sts, and fasten off.

SPECIAL NOTE: For children under three years of age, do not use any embellishments such as buttons, beads, pins, and the like, which may pose a danger. Use embroidery for eyes and other features.

Knitted cord, often called I-cord, is easy to make and can be used in a variety of ways. To make it, use dpn (of a size suitable for the yarn) to cast on the required number of stitches (3-5 stitches is a useful number). Knit all the stitches. Don't turn the needle. Slide the stitches to the other end of the needle and knit, pulling the yarn tightly across the back. Repeat until the cord is the desired length. Bind off all the stitches, or cut the yarn, thread a large-eyed needle and draw up the stitches tightly. Fasten off.

Candyfloss Shrug and Headband

A little touch of glamour for a special occasion, this kitten-soft set is sure to be a girl's favorite. The shrug is knitted sideways from sleeve edge to sleeve edge, then stitches are picked up around the body for the band. The headband, which you can whip up in an evening, is made from the remaining yarn.

SHRUG

Sizes

3–6 (8–10) years

Finished Measurements

Length: 9 (10)"/23 (25.5)cm

Sleeve seam: 2 (3)"/5 (7.5)cm

Materials

Approx total: 168yd/154m light worsted weight yarn in A and 137yd/125m novelty yarn (light worsted weight) in B

Knitting needles: size 4.5mm (U.S. 7) and size 5 mm (8 U.S.) or size needed to obtain gauge

Circular knitting needle: size 4.5.mm (U.S. 7), 24"/61cm long

Stitch holders

Ribbon of your choice

Tapestry needle

Gauge

17 sts and 25 rows = 4"/10cm in St st using A and larger needles

Always take time to check gauge.

Pattern Stitch

(8 row repeat)

Rows 1–4: With A, St st

Row 5 (RS): With B, k

Row 6: With B, k

Row 7: With B, p

Row 8: With B, k

Instructions

NOTE: Carry the yarn not in use loosely along the side of work.

Using larger needles and A, CO 56 (68) sts. Work 6 (10) rows in St st (counting CO row as Row 1).

Eyelet Row (RS): K3, *yo, k2tog, k2; rep from * to last st, k1.

Work 3 more rows in St st.

Place 9 (12) sts on holders at beg of next 2 rows—38 (44) sts rem.

Join in B and work straight in pat st, starting with Row 5, until piece measures approx 11 (13)"/28 (33) cm from CO edge, ending with Row 8 of the pat sequence.

Cut B.

Using A, CO 9 (12) sts at beg of next 2 rows—56 (68) sts.

Work 3 more rows in St st.

Work Eyelet Row as before.

Work 6 (10) rows in St st.

BO all sts.

FINISHING

Sew sleeve seams.

BAND

With RS facing, slip 18 (24) sts from holders at first sleeve seam onto circular needle.

Join in A, then k these sts and pick up and k a total of approx 120 (136) sts all around body of shrug, including the 18 (24) CO sts at the second sleeve seam.

Join and work around in k1, p1 rib for 1½"/4cm.

BO loosely in rib.

HEADBAND

Cut ribbon to the desired length and thread through eyelets.

Draw up to fit the upper arm comfortably and tie a bow.

Darn in loose ends.

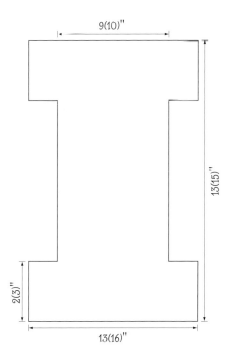

Finished Measurements

Circumference: 18 (20)"/ 45.5(51)cm

EXPERIENCE LEVEL

Easy

Pattern Stitch

(6 row repeat)

Row 1: With B, k

Row 2: With B, k

Row 3: With B, p

Row 4: With B, k

Row 5: With A, k

Row 6: With A, p

Instructions

Using larger needles and A, CO 80 (90) sts. K 2 rows.

Join in B. Work 2 reps of 6-row pat (12 rows).

Work Rows 1–4 once more.

Cut B.

Using A, k 2 rows.

BO loosely.

FINISHING

Sew seam.

Darn in loose ends.

THESE PROJECTS WERE MADE WITH:

2 balls of Lion Brand's *Lion Cashmere Blend*, 72% merino wool/15% nylon/3% cashmere, 1½oz/40g = 84yd/71m in #101 (light pink) (A) 1 ball of Lion Brand's *Tiffany*, 100% nylon, 1¾oz/50g = 137yd/ 125m in #101 (soft pink) (B)

This bright and cheerful set knits up quickly and can span the seasons. The cap-sleeved vest has a single button closure and contrast color piping, while the buttoned back vent detailing adds interest and a sophisticated note. The styling allows the growing child to get more wear from the vest—from hip length to just skimming the waist. The hat and scarf can top it all off or be worn separately.

Three's a Charm Set

Sizes

3 (4, 6, 8, 10) years

Finished Measurements

Chest: 26 (27, 28, 30, 32)"/66
  (68.5, 71, 76, 81.5)cm

Length: 13 (14½, 15½, 17½,
  19½)"/33 (37, 39.5, 44.5, 49.5)cm

Materials

Approx total: 171 (228, 228, 285,
  285)yd/156 (208, 208, 260,
  260)m in A and 57yd/52m in B
  bulky weight yarn

Knitting needles: size 8 mm (11
  U.S.) *or size needed to
  obtain gauge*

Circular knitting needles: size 8
  mm (11 U.S.), 16"/40cm long,
  and size 7 mm (10 1/2 U.S.),
  24"/61cm long

Stitch holders

Tapestry needle

One 1"/2.5cm button

Three ½"/1cm buttons

Snap fastener

Gauge

10 sts and 14 rows = 4"/10cm in
  rev St st using larger needles

Always take time to check gauge.

VEST

Pattern Stitch

(Rev St st)

Row 1(RS): P

Row 2: K

Rep rows 1 and 2

Instructions

BACK
*(worked in two pieces for the depth
of the vent)*

First Piece

With smaller needles and
  A, CO 21 (22, 23, 24, 25)
  sts. K 8 rows (4 garter st
  ridges).

Change to larger needles.

Next row (RS): P to last 5 sts, k5.

Cont in rev St st and k5 on every
  row for back vent until piece
  measures 5"/12.5cm from beg,
  ending with a RS row.

Next row (WS): BO 5 sts at beg of
  row and place the rem 16 (17, 18,
  19, 20) sts on a holder.

Second Piece

With smaller needles and A, CO 16
  (17, 18, 19, 20) sts. K 8 rows (4
  garter st ridges)

Change to larger needles.

Next row (RS): K5, p to end of row.

K5 sts for back vent and rem sts in
  rev St st until piece measures
  5"/12.5cm from beg, ending with
  a RS row.

Joining row (WS): K to end of row, place sts from holder onto needle and work across these sts, keeping the BO sts at the back of work—32 (34, 36, 38, 40) sts.

Cont in rev St st until back measures 7½ (8½, 9, 10½, 12)"/19 (21.5, 23, 26.5, 30.5) cm from beg.

Place underarm markers.

Cont until piece measures 13 (14½, 15½, 17½, 19½)"/33 (37, 39.5, 44.5, 49.5)cm from beg.

Place 10 (10, 11, 11, 12) sts on a holder for shoulder, 12 (14, 14, 16, 16) sts on a holder for back neck, and rem 10 (10, 11, 11, 12) sts on a holder for second shoulder.

FRONT
NOTE: Refer to page 16 for information on reversing the shaping on left and right front.

With smaller needles and A, CO 16 (17, 18, 19, 20) sts. K 8 rows (4 garter st ridges).

Change to larger needles. Work in rev St st until piece measures 7½ (8½, 9, 10½, 12)"/19 (21.5, 23.5, 26.5, 30.5)cm from beg, ending with a WS row.

Neck Shaping
Dec 1 st at neck edge every 2 rows, 4 (5, 4, 6, 8) times, then every 4 (4, 4, 4, 0) rows, 2 (2, 3, 2, 0) times—10 (10, 11, 11, 12) sts.

Cont until piece measures 13 (14½, 15½, 17½, 19½)"/33 (37, 39.5, 44.5, 49.5)cm from beg.

Place sts on a holder for shoulder seams.

FINISHING
Place shoulder sts on separate needles.

With WS facing, join fronts and back with a 3-needle BO.

Armbands
With RS facing, using smaller circular needle and B, pick up and k approx 34 (36, 38, 40, 42) sts around armhole edge.

K 1 row.

Cut B, join in A. K 4 rows.

Cut A, join in B. K 1 row.

BO loosely in B.

Seam sides and armbands.

Neckband
With RS facing, using smaller circular needle and B, starting at bottom of right front, pick up and knit 20 (23, 24, 28, 32) sts to beg of neck shaping, 15 (17, 18, 20, 21) sts along right neck edge, 12 (14, 14, 16, 16) sts from back neck holder, 15 (17, 18, 20, 21) sts along left neck edge, and 20 (23, 24, 28, 32) sts along left front—82 (94, 98, 112, 122) sts.

K 1 row.

Cut B, join in A. K 4 rows.

Cut A, join in B. K 1 row.

BO loosely in B.

Sew large button in middle of right front band with the snap fastener underneath it.

Sew second part of fastener in position on left front band.

To finish back vent, lap

upper part of vent over BO sts of the underlay and stitch down neatly on WS.

Sew 3 buttons in place to secure vent.

Darn in all loose ends.

HAT

Sizes

Approx 3–6 (8–10) years

Materials

Approx total: 57yd/52m each in A, B, C, and D bulky weight yarn

Knitting needles: size 7 mm (10½ U.S.)

Circular knitting needle: size 8 mm (11 U.S.) or size needed to obtain gauge

Gauge

10 sts and 14 rnds = 4"/10cm in St st using larger needles

Always take time to check gauge.

Stripe Sequence

NOTE: Worked over 12 garter st rows (6 garter st ridges).

Rows 1–2: B

Rows 3–4: A

Rows 5–6: B

Rows 7–8: D

Rows 9–10: B

Rows 11–12: C

Rep Rows 1–12

NOTE: Do not cut yarns not in use on striped sections but carry them loosely along side of work.

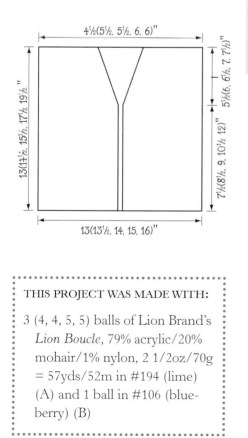

THIS PROJECT WAS MADE WITH:

3 (4, 4, 5, 5) balls of Lion Brand's *Lion Boucle*, 79% acrylic/20% mohair/1% nylon, 2 1/2oz/70g = 57yds/52m in #194 (lime) (A) and 1 ball in #106 (blueberry) (B)

EXPERIENCE LEVEL
Intermediate

Instructions

HATBAND

Using smaller needles and B, CO 14 sts. Work in garter st stripe sequence until 8 reps have been worked, taking care to end your stripe sequence correctly (48 garter st ridges).

To finish hatband, you may BO sts when the stripe sequence is complete and sew the two edges together into a circle. Or, slip a third needle through the CO loops of hatband, place the sts WS together, and work a 3-needle BO.

CROWN

With WS of hatband facing, using larger (circular) needle and B, pick up and k48 sts along the edge where you carried the yarns. Place a marker and k in rnds until crown measures 4 (5)"/10 (12.5)cm.

FINISHING

Slip 24 sts onto each of 2 needles. Place sts RSs together and BO using a third needle. Cut yarn, draw it through last rem st, and fasten off securely.

Weave in all loose ends.

Fold up the hatband.

THIS PROJECT WAS MADE WITH:

1 ball each of Lion Brand's *Lion Boucle*, 79% acrylic/20% mohair/1% nylon, 2½oz/70g = 57yds/52m in #194 (lime) (A), #106 (blueberry) (B), #112 (rose) (C), and #133 (tangerine) (D)

SCARF

Finished Measurements

Length: approx 54"/137cm

Width: 5"/1.25cm

Materials

Approx total: 57yd/52m each in A, B, C, and D bulky weight yarn

Knitting needles: size 8 mm (11 U.S.) or size needed to obtain gauge

Tapestry needle

Gauge

12 sts and 12 garter st ridges = 4"/10cm

Always take time to check gauge.

Stripe Sequence

NOTE: Worked over 12 garter st rows (6 garter st ridges).

Rows 1–2: B

Rows 3–4: A

Rows 5–6: B

Rows 7–8: D

Rows 9–10: B

Rows 11–12: C

Rep Rows 1–12

NOTE: Scarf is worked entirely in garter st. Striped bands alternate with 6"/15cm sections of solid color.

Do not cut yarns not in use on striped sections, but carry them loosely along side of work.

Instructions

Using B, CO 14 sts. K 1 row (CO row counts as first row).

Work in Stripe Sequence as given twice.

Work 2 rows in B.

Cut all yarns, except A.

Using A, work in garter st for 6"/15cm.

Join in B and cont, alternating 24 rows of Stripe Sequence and 6"/15cm of solid sections of D, C, and B, until a total of 5 striped sections, and 4 solid sections have been worked.

BO all sts.

FINISHING

Darn in all yarn ends neatly on WS.

> EXPERIENCE
> LEVEL
> ....
> **Easy**

THIS PROJECT WAS MADE WITH:

1 ball each of Lion Brand's *Lion Boucle,* 79% acrylic/20% mohair/1% nylon, 2½ oz/70g = 57yd/52m) in #194 (lime) (A), #106 (blueberry) (B), #112 (rose) (C), and #133 (tangerine) (D)

The combination of color, texture, and detailing of this tank all add up to a simply delicious design. Girls can layer this top over a blouse or under a little jacket, or wear it with crisp white shorts, cutoffs, or jeans for a summer-fresh look. With only two pieces to knit and very little finishing required, this pretty top will knit up in a flash.

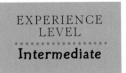

EXPERIENCE
LEVEL
· · · · · · · · · · · ·
Intermediate

Orange Sherbet Tank

Sizes

3 (4, 6, 8, 10) years

Finished Measurements

Chest: 26 (27, 28, 30, 32)"/66 (68.5, 71, 76, 81.5)cm

Length: 12 (13½, 14½, 16½, 18½)"/30.5 (34.5, 37, 42, 47)cm

Materials

Approx total: 246 (328, 328, 410, 410)yd/225 (300, 300, 375, 375)m worsted weight yarn

Knitting needles: size 5 mm (8 U.S.) or size needed to obtain gauge

Crochet hook: size H/5 mm (8 U.S.)

Stitch holders

Tapestry needle

Gauge

14 sts and 23 rows = 4"/10cm in St st

Always take time to check gauge.

Pattern Stitch

(multiple of 10 sts plus 1)

Row 1 (RS): K1, *(yo, k3, SK2P, k3, yo, k1); rep from * to end

Row 2: P

Rep Rows 1–2

Instructions

BACK

CO 51 (51, 51, 61, 61) sts. K 3 rows.

Work in pat st for 3"/7.5 cm, ending with pat Row 1.

K 3 rows.

Beg working in St st and adjust number of sts as follows:

1st size: Dec 1 st at beg and end of row.

3rd size: Inc 1 st at beg and end of row.

4th size: Dec 5 sts evenly across row.

NOTE: There will be 49 (51, 53, 56, 61) sts on the needle.

Cont working in St st until piece measures 7½ (8½, 9, 10½, 12)"/19 (21.5, 23, 26.5, 30.5)cm from beg, ending with a WS row.

Armhole Shaping

BO 4 (4, 4, 4, 5) sts at beg of next 2 rows.

Dec 1 st at each armhole edge on next and every other row, 2 (2, 2, 2, 3) times more—35 (37, 39, 42, 43) sts.

Cont in St st until piece measures 10 (11½, 12½, 14½, 16½)"/25.5 (29, 31.5, 37, 42)cm from beg, ending with a WS row.

Neck Shaping

Next row (RS): Work 8 (8, 10, 10, 11) sts, join in a new ball of yarn, BO 19 (21, 19, 22, 21) sts, then work to end of row.

Working both sides at the same time, dec 1 st at each neck edge on next and every other row, 1 (1, 1, 1, 2) times.

Work straight until piece measures 12 (13½, 14½, 16½, 18½)"/30.5 (34.5, 37, 42, 47)cm from beg, ending with a WS row.

Leave rem 6 (6, 8, 8, 8) sts on each shoulder on separate holders.

FRONT

Work as for back until piece measures 9 (10½, 11½, 13½, 16½)"/23 (26.5, 29, 34.5, 42)cm from beg, ending with a WS row.

Neck Shaping

Next row (RS): Work 12 (13, 14, 15, 15) sts, join in a new ball of yarn, BO 11 (11, 11, 12, 13) sts, then work to end of row.

Working both sides at the same time, BO 2 sts at each neck edge 2 times.

Dec 1 st at each neck edge every other row, 2 (3, 2, 3, 3) times.

Work straight until piece measures 12

(13½, 14½, 16½, 18½)"/30.5 (34.5, 37, 42, 47)cm from beg, ending with a WS row.

Leave rem 6 (6, 8, 8, 8) sts on each shoulder on separate holders.

FINISHING

Spray with water to block, taking care to pin the hem points out, and leave to dry.

Place each set of shoulder sts on separate needles and work a 3-needle BO.

Sew side seams.

Using crochet hook, work 1 row crab st (reverse single crochet) around neck and armhole edges.

Darn in loose ends.

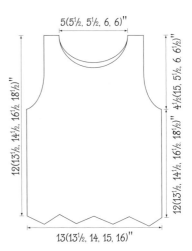

5(5½, 5½, 6, 6)"

12(13½, 14½, 16½, 18½)"

4½(15, 5½, 6, 6½)"

12(13½, 14½, 16½, 18½)"

13(13½, 14, 15, 16)"

THIS PROJECT WAS MADE WITH:

3 (4, 4, 5, 5) balls of Reynolds's *Blossom*, 50% acrylic/40% viscose/10% cotton, 1.75oz/50g = 82yd/75m in #3 (peach)

Kids in the Hoodie

Unusual tab fastenings and colorful buttons make quite an impact on this classic hooded jacket, which is worked in one piece to the underarm. The chunky yarn knits up quickly so that you soon get to the fun part— sorting through your button collection and picking the perfect ones.

99

Sizes

3(4,6,8) years

Finished Measurements

Chest: 26 (27, 29, 30)"/66 (68.5, 73.5, 76)cm

Length: 13 (14½, 15½, 17½)"/33 (37, 39.5, 45)cm

Materials

Approx total: 330 (440, 550, 550)yd/302 (402, 503, 503)m of a chunky weight yarn in A;

110yd/100m each in B, C, D

Knitting needles: 5 and 5.5mm (size 8 and 9 US), *or size to obtain gauge.*

Circular needle: 5mm (size 8 US), 24"/61cm long

NOTE: Circular needles will accommodate the sts more easily as the jacket is worked in one piece to the underarm, then the work is divided and the back and fronts are worked separately.

6 buttons for front tabs

1 button for back tab (optional)

6 x ⅝"/1.25cm snaps

Stitch holders

Stitch markers

Tapestry needle

Gauge

16 sts and 22 rows = 4"/10cm, measured over St st using larger needles

Always take time to check gauge.

Stripe Pattern

(worked over 12 rows in k1, p1 rib)

2 rows B

2 rows C

2 rows D

2 rows A

2 rows B

2 rows D

Instructions

BODY

Using smaller needles and A, CO 104 (108, 112, 120) sts. Change to B and work stripe pattern in k1, p1 rib for 1½ (2, 2, 2)"/4 (5, 5, 5)cm, carrying colors not in use loosely along the side of the work.

Cut all colors except A.

Change to larger needles. Work in St st until piece measures 7½ (8½, 9, 10½)"/19 (21.5, 23, 27.5)cm from beg.

(RS): K 26 (27, 28, 30) sts and place the rest of the sts on a holder.

RIGHT FRONT

Turn work and continue in St st until the piece measures 10½ (12, 13, 14)"/ 26.5 (30.5, 33, 3.5)cm from the beg.

Begin neck shaping:

(RS): K 4 (5, 5, 6) sts, place these on a holder and work to the end of the row.

Dec 1 st at neck edge every other row 5(5, 6, 6) times—17(17, 17, 18) sts.

Continue working until piece measures 13 (14½, 15½, 17½)"/33 (37, 39.5, 44.5)cm from beg.

Place the shoulder sts on a holder.

BACK

Place the next 52 (54, 56, 60) sts back onto the needle, join in the yarn and work until the piece measures 13 (14½, 15½, 17½)"/ 33 (37, 39.5, 44.5)cm from the beg.

Place 17 (17, 17, 18) sts at each side on separate holders for the shoulders.

Place the center 18 (20, 22, 24) sts on a holder.

LEFT FRONT

Sl the 26 (27, 28, 30) sts for the left front onto the needle, join in the yarn and complete to match the right front, reversing all shapings.

SLEEVES

Using the smaller needle, cast on 26 (28, 30, 32) sts and work the striped rib as given for the body for 1½ (2,2,2)"/4 (5, 5, 5)cm.

Change to the larger needle and A, and work in St st.

Inc 1 st on each side every 2 rows 4 (1, 0, 0) times, then every 4 rows 5 (9, 11, 12) times—44(48, 52, 56) sts.

Continue working straight until sleeve measures 7½(10, 11, 12½)"/ 19 (25.5, 28, 31.5)cm from beg.

BO the sts loosely.

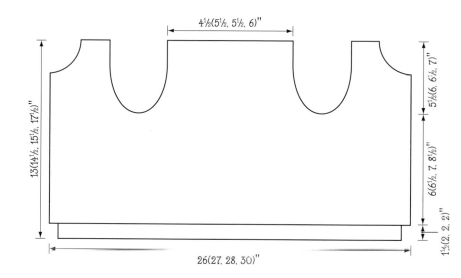

FINISHING

Block the knitting.

Sl each set of shoulder sts on separate needles and work a 3-needle bind off.

Hood

Using smaller needle and A, pick up and k 4(5, 5, 6) sts from holder at right front, pick up and k 10 (11, 12, 13) sts along right front neck, k the 18 (20, 22, 24)sts from the holder at back neck, pick up and k 10(11, 12, 13) sts along left front neck and k 4 (5, 5, 6) sts from holder at left front—46 (52, 56, 62) sts.

P 1 row.

K 21(24, 26, 29) sts, K into the back and front of the next 4 sts, K 21(24, 26, 29)—50 (56, 60, 66) sts.

Continue working in St st until the hood measures 7 (8, 8, 9)"/ 18 (20.5, 20.5, 23)cm.

Seam hood

Slip 25 (28, 30, 33) sts onto 2 separate needles and work a 3-needle BO.

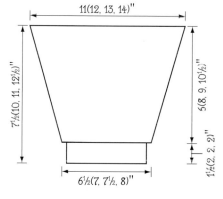

Front bands

Using the smaller circular needle, beg at the right lower edge with B, pick up and k 52 (58, 62, 70) sts along right front—70 (76, 76, 84) sts all around the edge of the hood, and 52 (58, 62, 70) sts along the left front—174 (192, 200, 224) sts.

Work 1"/2.5cm in the striped rib pattern.

Join in A and BO the sts loosely.

Sew sleeve seams.

Pin sleeves into armholes and seam.

Darn in loose ends.

The 1st at the start of the front neck shaping and the last ½"/1.3cm above the cast on edge of the bottom ribbing. Mark the 2nd tab evenly in between.

1st tab: Beg ½"/1.3cm from the right lower edge, using the smaller needle, and color of choice, pick up and k 5 sts from the BO sts of the front band. K 10 rows. BO the sts.

2nd tab (middle): To ensure that the tab is placed perfectly in the middle, pick up the 2 BO sts below the marker, so that the marked stitch becomes the 3rd st on the needle, pick up 2 sts on the other side of the marker. K 10 rows and BO.

3rd tab: To place the tab correctly, count 5 BO sts down from the neck edge, then pick up and k those 5sts for the tab as before.

Pin the tabs into their closed position on the left front band. Mark the positions of the opposite sets of tabs. Pick up sts and work the tabs as before.

Sew the male part of the snaps to the undersides of one set of button tabs.

Sew the buttons to the top of the tabs.

Sew the second part of the snaps in position on the opposite band.

Darn in loose ends.

TIP: Use a contrast color thread to sew on the buttons for an even more colorful effect; you can match it to the tabs if you like.

Back Tab (optional)

Using smaller needles and color of choice, CO 5 sts, K 10 rows. BO.

Pin in position on the back.

Secure by sewing on with a button.

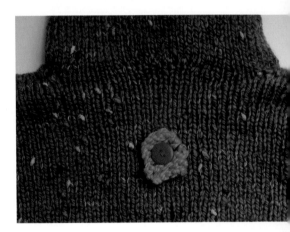

THIS PROJECT WAS MADE WITH:

Muench's *Tessin* (approx 110yds/100m) 3 (4, 5, 5) balls A # 822

All sizes: 1 ball each B #808, C #807, D #805

Button Tabs

NOTE: 5 sts for each tab are picked up from the BO sts of the front bands. Picking up stitches from the underside of the BO sts, so that the BO sts on the upper side of the bands are undisturbed creates a nice effect. Two dpns make it easier to knit the tabs, but are not essential.

Line up the opening edges of the jacket and mark the position of the tabs as follows:

Busy Bee Sweater and Hat Plus Variation

The textured honeycomb pattern is the star of this ensemble. Choose the rugged sweater and hat combo, or go for the layered look of the vest and headband. The sweater and vest are knit in the round to the armhole shaping. The hat brim has a contrast color lining to provide extra warmth. The headband can easily be made in an evening. All four pieces work equally well for a boy or girl.

EXPERIENCE
LEVEL
Experienced

Sizes

3 (4, 6, 8, 10) years

Finished Measurements

Chest: 26 (27, 29, 30, 32)"/66 (68.5, 73.5, 76, 81)cm

Length: 13 (14½, 15½, 17½, 19½")/33 (37, 39, 44.5, 49.5)cm

Materials

Approx total: 306 (459, 459, 612, 612)yd/ 279 (419, 419, 559, 559)m in A, 153yd/139m in B; 53yd/139m in C chunky weight yarn

Circular knitting needles (cn): 5.5 mm size (9 U.S), 24"/61cm long and 16"/40 cm long. and size 6.5mm (10½ U.S.), 24"/61 cm long, *or size needed to obtain gauge*

Set of double-pointed needles (dpns): size 6.5mm (10 U.S) (for hat) *or size to obtain gauge*

Stitch holders

Markers

Tapestry needle

NOTE: There will be sufficient yarn left over to make the ha.t

Gauge

14 sts and 18 rows = 4"/10cm in St st using larger needles

Always take time to check gauge.

SWEATER

NOTE: Special abbreviation for the pattern stitch

PUK (pick up and knit): with the right-hand needle, pick up the loop of B from the garter st row, 7 rows below, place the loop on the left-hand needle, and knit it together with the next st.

Pattern Stitch

(worked over 20 rounds)

Rnd 1: With B, k

Rnd 2: With B, p

Rnds 3–6: With C, k

Rnd 7: With B, k

Rnd 8: With B, p

Rnd 9: With A, *k5, puk; rep from * to end of rnd

Rnds 10–12: With A, k

Rnd 13: With B, k

Rnd 14: With B, p

Rnd 15: With C, k2, *puk, k5; rep from * to last 4 sts, puk, k3

Rnds 16–18: With C, k

Rnd 19: With B, k

Rnd 20: With B, p

Instructions

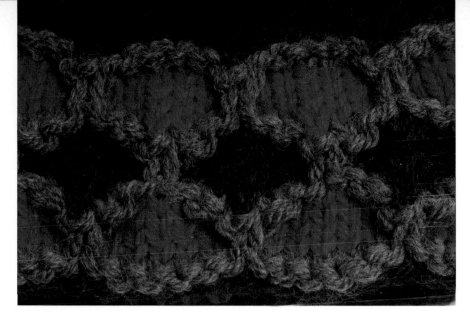

BODY

Using smaller cn and A, CO 90 (96, 102, 108, 112) sts and join, being careful not to twist the sts. Place a marker at the beg of the rnd and work k1, p1 rib for 1½ (2, 2, 2, 2)"/2 (6, 6, 6, 6)cm.

Change to larger circular needle.

Join in B and beg working the 20-row pat st (Cut and join in yarns as required or carry loosely twisted on the inside of the work at the beg of the rnds).

When the 20 pat rnds have been completed, cut B and C.

Next rnd: With A, repeat Rnd 9.

Cont knitting in A until the body measures 7½ (8½, 9, 10½, 12)"/19 (21.5, 23, 27, 30.5)cm from beg.

Divide For Front and Back

BACK

Next row (RS): K 45 (48, 51, 54, 56) sts, turn the work and place the rem sts on a holder.

Working back and forth in rows, continue in St st until the back measures

12 (13½, 14½, 16½, 18½)"/30.5 (34.5, 37, 42, 47) cm from beg, ending with a WS row.

Back neck shaping:

Next row (RS): Work 15 (15, 16, 17, 17) sts, join in a new ball of yarn, work 15 (18, 19, 20, 22) sts and place these on a holder for the back neck, work to end of row.

Working both sides at the same time, dec 1 st at each neck edge.

Cont working until the back measures 13 (14½, 15½, 17½, 19½)"/33 (37, 39, 44.5, 50)cm from CO edge.

Place the 14 (14, 15, 16, 16) shoulder sts on holders.

FRONT

Replace the sts on the needle and cont working as given for the back until the piece measures 10½ (12, 13, 14½, 16½)"/26 (30, 33, 37, 42)cm from beg, ending with a WS row.

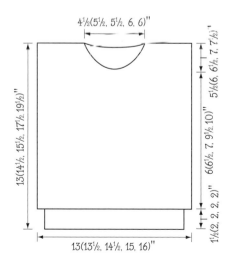

4½(5½, 5½, 6, 6)"

13(14½, 15½, 17½, 19½)"

5½(6, 6½, 7, 7½)"

6(6½, 7, 9½, 10)"

1½(2, 2, 2, 2)"

13(13½, 14½, 15, 16)"

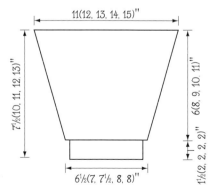

11(12, 13, 14, 15)"

7½(10, 11, 12, 13)"

6(8, 9, 10, 11)"

6½(7, 7½, 8, 8)"

1½(2, 2, 2, 2)"

Neck Shaping

Next row (RS): Work 18 (19, 19, 20, 21) sts, join in a new ball of yarn, work 9 (10, 13, 14, 14) sts and place these on a holder for the front neck, work to end of row.

Working both sides at the same time, dec 1 st at each neck edge 4 (5, 4, 4, 5) times.

Cont working until the front measures the same as the back to the shoulders.

Leave the 14 (14, 15, 16, 16) shoulder sts on holders.

SLEEVES

With smaller needle and A, CO 24 (24, 26, 28, 30) sts and work 1 1/2 (2, 2, 2, 2)"/2 (6, 6, 6, 6)cm back and forth in k1, p1 rib.

Change to larger needle and work 2 rows in St st.

Sleeve Shaping

Next row (RS): Inc 1 st on each side every 2 (2, 2, 0, 0) rows, 2 (2, 2, 0, 0) times, then every 4th row 5 (7, 8, 11, 11) times.

There will be 38 (42, 46, 50, 52) sts on the needle.

Cont working in St st until the sleeve measures 7½ (10, 11, 12, 13)"/19 (25, 28, 30, 33) cm

from beg.

BO loosely.

FINISHING

Block pieces.

Place each set of shoulder sts back on the needles and work a 3-needle BO.

NECKBAND

(RS): With smaller 16"/40cm circular needle and A, starting at the left shoulder, pick up and knit approx 8 (9, 9, 10, 10) sts along the left neck edge, k9 (10, 13, 14, 14) sts from the holder for the front neck, pick up and knit approx 8 (9, 9, 10, 10) sts along the right neck edge and 19 (22, 23, 24, 26) sts across the back, including the back neck sts left on the holder—approx 44 (50, 54, 58, 60) sts.

Work 1"/2.5cm in k1, p1 rib.

BO loosely in rib.

Sew sleeve seams.

Pin the tops of the sleeves into the armhole openings and stitch in place.

Darn in loose ends.

HAT

Finished Measurements

Circumference:
18 (20)"/45 (50)cm

Instructions

Using the smaller 16"/40cm circular
needle and C, loosely CO 54 (60)
sts.

Join into a rnd, being careful not to
twist the sts.

Place a marker to indicate the beg of
the rnds.

HEM

Work rnds in St st (k every row) for
2½"/6cm.

Change to larger 16"/40cm circular
needle and A.

K 1 row.

HEM FOLDLINE

P 1 row.

Work the 20-row pat st.

Cut B and C.

With A, repeat Rnd 9.

Work 3 more rnds in A.

Crown Shaping

1st dec rnd: *K7 (8), k2tog; repeat
from * to end of rnd.

Next and all even-numbered rnds:
K.

2nd dec rnd: *K6 (7), k2tog; repeat
from * to end of rnd.

3rd dec rnd: *K5 (6), k2tog; repeat
from * to end of rnd.

4th dec rnd: *K4 (5), k2tog; repeat
from * to end of rnd.

Cont working the decs in this manner every other rnd, changing to
dpn when it becomes necessary,
until 6 (6) sts rem.

Cut yarn, thread through the
remaining sts, and fasten off
securely.

FINISHING

Fold the hem to the inside along the
foldline.

Stitch in place.

Darn in loose ends.

EXPERIENCE
LEVEL

Experienced

THESE PROJECTS WERE MADE
WITH:

2 (3, 3, 4, 4) balls of Lion Brand's
Wool-Ease Chunky, 5.00 oz./
140 g (153 yd/140 m) 80%
Acrylic, 20% Wool = 153yd/
140m in #127 (walnut) (A), 1
ball of #115 (bay harbor) (B),
and 1 ball of #112 (red) (C)

VEST

Sizes

3 (4, 6, 8, 10) years

Finished Measurements

Chest: 26 (27, 29, 30, 32)"/66
(68.5, 73.5, 76, 81.5)cm

Length: 13 (14½, 15½, 17½,
19½)"/33 (37, 39.5, 44.5, 49.5)cm

Materials

Approx total: 286 (286, 429, 429,
429)yd/261 (261, 392, 392, 392)m
in A; 143yd/131m in B;
143yd/131m in C chunky
weight yarn

Circular knitting needles (cn): size
5.5 mm (9 U.S.), 24"/61cm long
and 16"/40cm long, and size 6.5
mm (10½ U.S.), 24"/61cm long,
or size needed to obtain gauge

Stitch holders

Stitch markers

Tapestry needle

NOTE: There will be sufficient
yarn left over to make the headband.

Gauge

14 sts and 20 rows = 4"/10cm in
St st with larger needles

Always take time to check gauge.

NOTE: Special abbreviation for the
pattern stitch

PUK (pick up and knit): With the
right-hand needle, pick up the
loop of B from the garter st row, 7
rows below, place the loop on the
left-hand needle, and knit it
together with the next stitch.

Pattern Stitch
••••••••••••••••••••••••••••••••
(worked over 20 rounds)

Rnd 1: With B, k

Rnd 2: With B, p

Rnds 3–6: With C, k

Rnd 7: With B, k

Rnd 8: With B, p

Rnd 9: With A, *k5, puk; repeat
from * to end of rnd

Rnds 10–12: With A, k

Rnd 13: With B, k

Rnd 14: With B, p

Rnd 15: With C, k2, *puk, k5; repeat
from * to the last 4 sts, puk, k3

Rnds 16–18: With C, k

Rnd 19: With B, k

Rnd 20: With B, p

HEADBAND

Instructions

BODY
Work as given for the body of the sweater (page 105).

FINISHING
Block pieces.

Place each set of shoulder sts on separate needles and work a 3-needle BO.

Neckband
Work as given for the sweater (page 105).

Armbands
With RS facing, using smaller 16"/40cm circular needle and A, beg at underarm, pick up and k approx 40 (44, 48, 52, 54) sts around armhole.

Work in k1, p1 rib for 1"/2.5cm.

BO all sts loosely in rib.

Darn in loose ends.

> **THE VEST AND HEADBAND WERE MADE WITH:**
>
> 2 (2, 3, 3, 3) balls of Plymouth Yarn's *Encore Chunky*, 75% acrylic/25% wool, 3.5oz/100g = 143yd/130m in #1386 (A), 1 ball of #1384 (B), and 1 ball of #1385 (C)

Finished Measurements
Circumference: 18 (20)"/45.5 (51)cm

Instructions

Using smaller 16"/40cm circular needle and A, loosely CO 54 (60) sts.

Join into a rnd, being careful not to twist the sts.

Place a marker to indicate the beg of rnds.

Work around in St st (k every rnd) for 1"/2.5cm for first half of headband lining.

Change to larger 16"/40cm circular needle and B.

Work 20 rnds of pat st.

Cut B and C.

With A, rep Rnd 9.

Change to smaller circular needle.

Work around in St st for 1"/2.5cm for second part of lining.

BO loosely.

FINISHING
Turn the two halves of the headband lining to the inside and seam together.

NOTE: If a snugger fit is desired, run a piece of elastic cut to size through the casing formed by the lining.

METRIC CONVERSIONS

INCHES	METRIC (MM/CM)	INCHES	METRIC (MM/CM)	INCHES	METRIC (MM/CM)
1/8	3 mm	8 1/2	21.6 cm	23	58.4 cm
3/16	5 mm	9	22.9 cm	23 1/2	59.7 cm
1/4	6 mm	9 1/2	24.1 cm	24	61 cm
5/16	8 mm	10	25.4 cm	24 1/2	62.2 cm
3/8	9.5 mm	10 1/2	26.7 cm	25	63.5 cm
7/16	1.1 cm	11	27.9 cm	25 1/2	64.8 cm
1/2	1.3 cm	11 1/2	29.2 cm	26	66 cm
9/16	1.4 cm	12	30.5 cm	26 1/2	67.3 cm
5/8	1.6 cm	12 1/2	31.8 cm	27	68.6 cm
11/16	1.7 cm	13	33 cm	27 1/2	69.9 cm
3/4	1.9 cm	13 1/2	34.3 cm	28	71.1 cm
13/16	2.1 cm	14	35.6 cm	28 1/2	72.4 cm
7/8	2.2 cm	14 1/2	36.8 cm	29	73.7 cm
15/16	2.4 cm	15	38.1 cm	29 1/2	74.9 cm
1	2.5 cm	15 1/2	39.4 cm	30	76.2 cm
1 1/2	3.8 cm	16	40.6 cm	30 1/2	77.5 cm
2	5 cm	16 1/2	41.9 cm	31	78.7 cm
2 1/2	6.4 cm	17	43.2 cm	31 1/2	80 cm
3	7.6 cm	17 1/2	44.5 cm	32	81.3 cm
3 1/2	8.9 cm	18	45.7 cm	32 1/2	82.6 cm
4	10.2 cm	18 1/2	47 cm	33	83.8 cm
4 1/2	11.4 cm	19	48.3 cm	33 1/2	85 cm
5	12.7 cm	19 1/2	49.5 cm	34	86.4 cm
5 1/2	14 cm	20	50.8 cm	34 1/2	87.6 cm
6	15.2 cm	20 1/2	52 cm	35	88.9 cm
6 1/2	16.5 cm	21	53.3 cm	35 1/2	90.2 cm
7	17.8 cm	21 1/2	54.6 cm	36	91.4 cm
7 1/2	19 cm	22	55 cm	36 1/2	92.7 cm
8	20.3 cm	22 1/2	57.2 cm	37	94.0 cm

ACKNOWLEDGMENTS

This book would not have been possible without my husband Ron and my daughters, Julia and Lucia.

I'm very grateful to Carol Taylor and the creative team at Lark; my editor Joanne O' Sullivan and associate editor Susan Kieffer, who pulled it all together; Dawn Cusick and Jane Lippmann who helped me in a great many ways; Stacey Budge, art director; Keith Wright, photographer; and all the lively, beautiful children who modeled for us: Athena, Bergen, Daniel, Elisabeth, Eva, Gillian, Haylie, Juliana, Keagan, Laney, Maeve, Margaret, Nikki, Sam, Seth, Shinky, Xavi and Zelda. My thanks and appreciation to the following yarn companies, who provided me with some of the yarns used in this book:

LION BRAND (LISA DENBERG AND CARLA HORVATH)

PLYMOUTH YARN COMPANY (JOANNE TURCOT)

COATS AND CLARK (KATHLEEN SAMS)

MUENCH YARNS

BERNAT

KNIT ONE, CROCHET TOO

Bibliography

Allen, Pam. *Knitting for Dummies.* New York: Hungry Minds, Inc., 2002.

Feitelson, Ann. *The Art of Fair Isle Knitting: History, Technique, Color, Patterns.* Loveland, CO: Interweave Press, 1997.

Stanley, Montse. *Knitter's Handbook.* New York: Reader's Digest Publishers, 1999.

Vogue Knitting, eds.. *Vogue Knitting: The Ultimate Knitting Book.* New York: Sixth&Spring Books, 2002.

INDEX